LORD, HAVE MERCY

LORD, HAVE MERCY

Praying for Justice with Conviction and Humility

Claire E. Wolfteich

JOSSEY-BASS
A Wiley Imprint
www.josseybass.com

Library of Congress Cataloging-in-Publication Data

Wolfteich, Claire E.
Lord, have mercy: praying for justice with conviction and humility / Claire E. Wolfteich.
p. cm.
Includes bibliographical references and index.
ISBN-13: 978-0-7879-8269-0 (cloth)
ISBN-10: 0-7879-8269-5 (cloth)
1. Prayer—Christianity. 2. Christianity and culture. I. Title.
BV210.3.W64 2006
248.3'2—dc22
2006019144

The Practices of Faith Series
Dorothy C. Bass, Series Editor

Practicing Our Faith:
A Way of Life for a Searching People
Dorothy C. Bass, Editor

Receiving the Day:
Christian Practices for Opening the Gift of Time
Dorothy C. Bass

Honoring the Body:
Meditations on a Christian Practice
Stephanie Paulsell

Testimony:
Talking Ourselves into Being Christian
Thomas G. Long

A Song to Sing, A Life to Live:
Reflections on Music as Spiritual Practice
Don Saliers, Emily Saliers

Lord, Have Mercy: Praying for Justice
with Conviction and Humility
Claire E. Wolfteich

In the Midst of Chaos: Caring for
Children as Spiritual Practice
Bonnie J. Miller-McLemore

For Jack, and for our children,
John Christopher, Hannah Alice,
and Thomas Paul

Contents

———

Editor's Foreword   ix

Preface   xv

Acknowledgments   xxi

Chapter 1 Prayer in an Election Year: Lord, Have Mercy   1

Chapter 2 A Cloud of Witnesses: Prayer and the Christian Way of Life   17

Chapter 3 Spirituality and Politics: Tensions Within a Congregation   33

Chapter 4 Praying in the Spirit of the Prophets: South Africa Under Apartheid   57

Chapter 5 Lament and Reconciliation: Praying Through Injustice   77

Chapter 6 Walking with Our Lady: Cesar Chavez and the Farm Workers   99

Chapter 7 Division in the Body: Prayer and Abortion   121

Chapter 8 Going to the Wellsprings of Trust: The Taizé Vision   145

Chapter 9 Praying with Conviction and Humility   163

Notes   183

The Author   197

Index   199

Editor's Foreword

———

Each morning's news brings fresh evidence of the suffering human beings impose on one another when justice does not shape our actions and relationships. Sometimes a report from Darfur or an account of a church-burning in my own country makes me catch my breath, which emerges a few seconds later as a whispered "Oh my God!" A prayer, I trust, is buried in this thoughtlessly uttered phrase, a seed of the prayer I will also address to God more deliberately later in the day, privately or in worship with others.

This is one of the things Christians do when we see injustice: we pray, pouring out to God our rage and compassion and longing, beseeching God to ensure that justice will soon overturn oppression. Prayers like these rise like incense from Christian people everywhere, including those gathered around the still-smoldering ashes of the church building mentioned in the morning news. We pray when injustice falls upon others, and we pray when we ourselves feel its crushing weight.

Saying such prayers aloud when we are not at home or at church feels increasingly difficult to many of us, however. For some, praying in the public square—where addressing matters of injustice almost always requires us to be—is intrinsically difficult in a pluralistic society. Others feel drawn to prayer even in the midst of public engagement but are put off by the ways in which some highly politicized religious leaders (or ostentatiously religious political leaders) seem to use prayer as a bludgeon against their enemies. With the intersection between religious practice and political justice so difficult to navigate, retreat becomes a ready option. Some take concern for social justice off the table and embrace a private spirituality that fails to address the needs of those who suffer poverty or oppression, while others gather in enclaves of the like-minded and make light of the difficulties perceived by their more cautious coreligionists.

In *Lord, Have Mercy,* Claire E. Wolfteich invites readers to think deeply about the difficulties we face when we pray for justice, not only in public but also within our own parishes and congregations and in the silence of our private prayers. Yet she also helps us to see the necessity of such prayer and its important place in Christian faith and life. She does this by setting us in the midst of people who have prayed for justice in communities all over the world in recent decades—and then by setting both them and us within the millennia-old practice of prayer as it has taken shape among our forebears in faith. Attentive readers will find here both an invitation to pray more faithfully and help in doing so.

I am delighted to add *Lord, Have Mercy: Praying for Justice with Conviction and Humility* to the Practices of Faith series, which offers wisdom drawn from the deep wells of Christian belief and experience to those who long to live with integrity in today's rapidly changing world. The series's initial book, *Practicing Our Faith: A Way of Life for a Searching People,* found such wisdom in twelve practices that shape a way of life attuned to God's presence and the well-being of all: honoring the body, hospitality, household economics, saying yes and saying no, keeping Sabbath, discernment, testimony, shaping communities, forgiveness, healing, dying well, and singing our lives to God. By participating in these practices together over time, Christian people address fundamental human needs in ways that reflect and respond to God's grace to them and to the whole world in Jesus Christ. Each subsequent book in the series has focused on one of the practices that received only a single chapter's exploration in *Practicing Our Faith.*

Lord, Have Mercy takes the series in a seemingly new direction. Rather than focusing on one of the practices in *Practicing Our Faith,* this book explores how another practice—the practice of prayer—has been embodied in several actual communities in times of historic confrontation with social injustice. In fact, prayer and the yearning for justice are woven into the entire fabric of the life-giving way of life advocated by the series as a whole. Every Christian practice is infused with the attentive relationship with God that is at the heart of prayer. And any Christian practice that demeans just relationships among people fails to address fundamental human needs and reflect God's grace. Moreover, the virtues of conviction and humility emphasized by Wolfteich are vital not only to praying for justice but to other practices as well. Testimony or healing performed by those who lack humility would be unlikely to reflect God's grace, while hospitality or forgiveness performed without conviction would be unlikely to open doors that are presently blocked by hostility.

Editor's Foreword

By emphasizing these dimensions of the Christian life, Claire E. Wolfteich helps us to see that all the practices of faith are most vital and authentic when the web of relationship among them is strong. No faithful practice can exist in isolation from other practices. As we learn in this book, the South Africans who prayed for justice also became involved in the difficult and strenuous practices of forgiveness, dying well, and saying yes and saying no. Similarly, the prayer of the Taize Community clearly goes hand in hand with hospitality, Sabbath, and singing our lives to God.

The focus of *Lord, Have Mercy* on specific communities of practice also sheds light on a dynamic that is described but never fleshed out in *Practicing Our Faith*: Christian practices endure across centuries and across cultures, but each living community of faith must figure out how to embody these practices faithfully in its own social and cultural context. The communities described here participate in practices bequeathed to them by centuries of earlier practitioners, but conflict about how to engage in these practices sometimes erupts as they move into an uncertain future—a congregation fights bitterly, a nation is deeply divided. Meanwhile, in these same communities and others—at Taize and among the farmworkers of California, for example—creativity also breaks forth as practitioners craft forms of prayer that address the brokenness of church and society. In comprehending how the communities of faith we meet here responded to the challenges and opportunities of their time, we begin to ponder how we engage in Christian practices in our own communities as well.

By sharing her own struggles with this practice and providing theological reflection on historical and biblical patterns of prayer at the book's beginning and end, Claire E. Wolfteich honors the complexity and uncertainty of this practice while also helping readers to make it our own. As you explore these pages and consider how you may grow as one who prays in and for a world that is daily wracked by the suffering and despair that flow from injustice, I encourage you to find companions with whom to discuss, pray about, and live this practice and the other practices that comprise a way of life attuned to God's presence and the well-being of all. To assist you in this endeavor, other resources on Christian practices, including a *Guide for Learning, Conversation, and Growth* based on this book, are available at www.practicingourfaith.org.

August 2006 DOROTHY C. BASS
Valparaiso, Indiana Editor, Practices of Faith Series

Preface

Lord, Have Mercy:
Praying for Justice with
Conviction and Humility

———

Probably we all have had the experience of reading the newspaper and becoming a little depressed—so much bad news, so many seemingly insurmountable problems. We may have wondered how to make sense of some of the stories we read. How do we respond to yet more deaths in Iraq? Should we support stem cell research? Then there are the issues very close to home: How to respond to violence in our own neighborhoods, to layoffs in a local corporation, to abuse in our own church?

We may find ourselves in a quandary. On the one hand, we want our faith to be engaged with the world around us—to have something to say, to guide us in our actions in society, to make a difference. On the other hand, we may be leery about how religion gets woven into social and political life—in empty or even dangerous rhetoric, in powerful lobbying, in public displays of piety that seem simply hypocritical or self-serving. What would it mean to witness to our faith and raise up our concerns to God in ways that express conviction yet also care and humility?

I am a student and teacher of Christian spirituality. Many of the great spiritual teachers in the tradition try to show us how to draw closer to God in prayer; prayer seems to be at the core of a Christian way of life. Yet much of this spiritual guidance has little to say about social issues, politics, economics, or any such "worldly" matters. I have struggled to recover wisdom that helps us see the holiness of those mundane spheres—our families, our work, even the messy business of creating laws and policies for the common good. This book is an outgrowth of my desire to both mine the spiritual riches of the tradition and pay attention to the very real, complicated lives of laypersons today. In particular, I wanted to explore how communities pray about social issues, especially where questions of justice are at stake but also where opinions about what constitute that justice or what is an appropriate public faith witness are divided. How do people pray? What language do they find? How do they navigate diverse opinions on these questions, and how do they (or do they not) check their own certainties? What theological and spiritual dilemmas arise in their stories, and how do we grapple with these dilemmas as we step into their stories?

For many of us, prayer can be difficult to connect to the complicated social problems around us. We may feel that spirituality should be somehow different, in another realm or compartment from the controversial or incomprehensible events of our day. We may be members of a congregation that prays quite specifically—too specifically, perhaps—for particular political outcomes. We may be disturbed to see that worship can actually cause division, alienation, and manipulation in our own faith community.

Or we may be put off by the many examples of political and religious leaders who use prayer as a tool to advance their own agenda, who seem so certain that God is on their side. We may be rightly cautious that prayer should not lose a sense of humility and connection with mystery.

On the other hand, some of us may be passionate advocates for social change. We may see no disconnect between our faith and our efforts for justice. We yearn, though, for models and guides to help us be better witnesses. We also may find that in our intense action we have become spiritually dry, perhaps lost the ability or desire to pray. We know that we need to be renewed spiritually, and we hope to find a way to better integrate prayer with action for social justice.

This book is for all who would echo the question posed by the disciple in Luke 11:1: "Lord, teach us how to pray." It is for anyone who seeks to thoughtfully connect faith with political, social, and economic issues. It is for those who want to grow in discernment of God's purposes in the world, who want to stand on the side of justice, and who want to pray. I hope that the book will be useful to faith communities that seek to better integrate spiritual nurture and social justice witness. Some of those communities have not given much energy to sociopolitical questions; for others, their mission is defined by these questions. Some have a social justice committee and a spiritual life committee that barely talk to one another. As I work with pastors and teach in a graduate school of theology, my experience tells me that it will be particularly valuable for people preparing for or engaged in public and religious leadership to wrestle with this book.

Over the past several years I have talked with many people about how their prayer leads them to engagement with social issues, or how their concern for social justice takes shape in their prayer. These conversations have been rich and thought-provoking, raising many questions, sometimes inspiring me. As I work in spiritual and pastoral formation and teach theology, I keep searching for more resources to guide us in how to pray. Though encouraged that a few recent works of scholarship have looked anew at the relationship between spiritual traditions and social transformation, I have found very few resources that grapple concretely with questions about prayer and social justice. Some offer a theoretical discussion of the nature of prayer, without sufficient attention to the complexities of actual practice; other authors tend toward the inspirational, without leaving enough room for readers to enter into the difficult theological questions imbedded in various practices. What I hope to do in this book is allow stories of actual practice to open up a much-needed conversation about how to pray in ways that are attentive to social justice, yet reflective and humble. I do not present easy answers; rather, I guide diverse readers to come to their own clarity and renewed practice through wrestling with the stories and dilemmas presented here, seeing how people in each situation found their way into prayer, in some cases learning to pray with them.

As I have engaged students with these stories, what is particularly fascinating is to see how each story evokes theological and political responses, clarifying beliefs, inviting readers into varied ways of praying. For example, some students who concluded that the bold prayer of anti-apartheid leaders in South Africa was entirely necessary in that context, and who found farm worker organizer Cesar Chavez's seamless integration of piety and protest inspiring and authentic, called the work of prayer in pro-life rallies outside of abortion clinics "spectacle" and "performance." Why? Juxtaposing these stories enables us to look more deeply at our own practices of prayer and our assumptions about prayer. How do we practice petitionary prayer in the face of persistent evil? How to pray in and on behalf of a community of people who have diverse views on social issues? When does public prayer become a political tool rather than authentic witness? How might contemplative prayer be a reconciling witness in the world? I invite readers to enter with me into these stories. My hope is that the book will engage, challenge, and transform, and that it will spark a searching and fruitful conversation.

Acknowledgments

This book has its roots in a grant project that I codirected from 1997 to 2006, "Church and Theology in the Contemporary World," generously funded by the Lilly Endowment. I gratefully acknowledge their support as well as the invaluable input of my codirector, Peter Berger, who has throughout energized and informed this work. Much of the research for the book originated in and was supported by this grant project. I also acknowledge the many colleagues who have participated in conferences that we organized and hosted along the way; they provided useful insights into the topic of prayer and social engagement from diverse international perspectives.

The Valparaiso Project on the Education and Formation of People in Faith also supported the writing of this book, and to the project and its director, Dorothy C. Bass, I express profound gratitude. Many thanks to her and also to Sheryl Fullerton, editor at Jossey-Bass, for their careful reading of the manuscript and very thoughtful feedback. They have been wonderful dialogue partners and a pleasure to work with throughout the process.

Students in various classes I teach at Boston University School of Theology have grappled with some of the stories in this book, and for their thoughts and feedback I am grateful. I am particularly indebted to a number of graduate student assistants who provided excellent research assistance, among them most recently Nicole Johnson and Kirk VanGilder.

Finally, I wish to thank my family, including my sister Phyllis, who helped make some of the international research possible, and my husband, Jack, for his constant love and support. And John, Hannah, and Thomas for lightening my spirit.

LORD,
HAVE
MERCY

Chapter 1

PRAYER IN AN ELECTION YEAR: LORD, HAVE MERCY

———

I remember clearly how I felt on Election Day, 2004. I sat in my car outside the voting booth, still not decided about how to vote. I had read up on the presidential candidates, watched the debates, and talked it over with friends and family. Still, neither John Kerry nor George W. Bush emerged as the clear choice.

I was struggling to put the decision in a faith perspective. I heard many people doing it, simply, with ease. Some were liberal Christians, certain that God would want to banish George W. Bush from the presidency, stop the war in Iraq, and expand funding for social welfare. Others were conservative Christians, certain that God needed Bush to uphold the moral fiber of the nation, foster democracy and freedom abroad, limit abortion, and stop the movement for gay marriage.

As I, a Roman Catholic, looked at the two major candidates, I saw neither perspective completely embodying my values, my faith. I wondered if my faith had much to do with the election. I haltingly tried to pray for wisdom but felt a real disconnect. Did God have a side in this election? Surely—yet neither choice sat well. No clear sign emerged. No lightning bolts flashed. I was sure that God's purposes aligned with some of the aims of each candidate, but on other issues the fit was murkier. In the end, I made the best choice I could and, on leaving the voting booth, simply prayed: Lord, have mercy.

Although we may not have been publicized as much as the more vocal and more certain voters, I imagine many people of faith found themselves in a somewhat similar position: wanting to relate their beliefs to this practical decision, yet unclear about precisely how faith would direct this choice. Just a bit less sure that God saw politics through the same lens that we did. Just a little suspicious of how others—conservatives and liberals—so easily heard God's voice.

We believe that our faith should make a difference, that we should be able to connect our spiritual life with concrete issues in the world around us. Yet it can be quite difficult to do so with real thought and fidelity. Complicated social questions may seem simply disconnected from our faith. We often unabashedly make God the spokesperson for our own viewpoint. Sometimes our best efforts to bring a faith perspective to social questions cause division within the communities we hold dear. So, how do we enter faithfully into the events, debates, and questions of public life?

PRAYER AT THE HEART

I want to focus on one aspect of that large question: prayer. Prayer is at the heart of the life of faith. It is a natural part of relating to a God on whom we depend and with whom we are called to intimacy. If we believe God cares deeply about the world, then it is natural also to lift up to God all those conflicts, dilemmas, and struggles woven into our common human life. How, though, do we pray thoughtfully, faithfully, about social and political questions?

You may wonder why I have chosen to focus on prayer. There are, of course, other practices—such as lobbying, volunteering, preaching, and educating—that relate faith to social and political life. Many Christians distribute food to the poor, visit the sick, and give money to charity. Church social action groups join in political protest, lead antiviolence campaigns, conduct voter registration drives, and work for legislation that squares with their religious beliefs. These are important ways to embody faith in our society as neighbors and citizens. Prayer without such action would not be sufficient.

Nevertheless, prayer has been at the heart of Christians' shared life of faith from the beginnings of the Christian community. In his earliest surviving letter, for example, Paul encouraged the Christian community at Thessalonica to persevere in faith. Paul cared greatly for these new converts and expressed joy that they were standing "firm in the Lord" (1 Thessalonians 3:8), living the gospel he had preached to them. They faced persecution, however, and Paul feared his beloved community would weaken. Prevented from returning to the city, Paul prayed to be with them: "Night and day we pray most earnestly that we may see you face to face and restore whatever is lacking in your faith" (1 Thessalonians 3:10). As they faced opposition, Paul counseled them to "rejoice always, pray without ceasing, give thanks in all circumstances; for this is the will of God in Christ Jesus for you" (1 Thessalonians 5:16–18). In Paul's eyes, prayer is not limited to discrete moments set aside from the rest of our lives. Rather, he encourages Christians to pray without ceasing and always in a context of thanksgiving. Petitionary and intercessory prayer then flow from that way of living. Paul implored the Thessalonians to pray for him and for his fellow evangelists Silvanus and Timothy. In Paul's understanding, prayer gave a struggling church strength and wove Christians—even though separated by distance and persecutions—together in bonds of love and shared faith.

Prayer is the glue and the ground for the life of the Christian community. It binds the church together and keeps it centered in the power of the Holy Spirit. After the death and resurrection of Jesus, the disciples—who must have been perplexed, amazed, and frightened—gathered in a room in Jerusalem, awaiting the return of Jesus and the power of the Holy Spirit that Jesus had promised them: "All these were constantly devoting themselves to prayer, together with certain women, including Mary the mother of Jesus, as well as his brothers" (Acts 1:14). We see the early community spending much time in the Temple, breaking bread together in their homes, praising and praying to God (Acts 2:42, 46–47). It is this rootedness in prayer that Paul and his followers desire for the fledgling church. The letter to the Ephesians counsels: "Pray in the Spirit at all times in every prayer and supplication. To that end keep alert and always persevere in supplication for all the saints" (Ephesians 6:18–19). Prayer, then, is the first "action" we do for one another. It also expresses who we are. If social action is to spring from and reflect Christian faith, it must be rooted first in our life as a community of prayer.

This does not mean prayer is a private "churchy" practice separate from the larger world. Rather, it is a public practice of a community that is very much in this world, attending to its suffering and seeking to live out the gospel amid the complexities of particular social situations.

A RUNNING REMINDER: BE STILL

Though it may be at the heart of faith, prayer is still not easy. Contemporary Western culture encourages us to be productive, get moving, not waste time. Success is measured by what we do, how much we do, how many hours we put in at work. Prayer can be difficult in the face of these cultural messages. It is countercultural to wait, contemplate, sit still.

When I began teaching at the university where I continue to work now, I arrived after a period of whirlwind activity. I had just graduated with my doctoral degree, moved halfway across the country to a city where I knew nobody, piled my boxes into a bare apartment, and tried to set up my office. I would be meeting new students and new colleagues, running from one meeting to the next, and deciphering the ins and outs of working on this campus. Instinctively, I knew I needed some spiritual reminder to center me in my workspace. I chose this Scriptural passage: "Be still and know that I am God" (Psalm 46:10). I decided to create a screensaver on my computer with a shorthand message: "Be still. . . ." With great satisfaction, I set up the words in bold red print. I sat back and watched the screensaver, preparing for a prayerful moment. The bold red words *Be still* went racing across my computer screen, over and over again. The running screensaver contradicted its own message! The worst part is, the irony did not even hit me until months later, when I finally noticed the contradiction. I left it as is, because it seemed to deftly point out the difficulty of being still in a running culture, with a running personality.

PRAYER AS PAUSE BUTTON

I have come to realize that even if prayer can seem as though it is slowing me down (what I really want to do is hop into bed, or finish this chapter, or clean up the dishes), ultimately prayer is not in tension with action. It is instead a kind of pause button, so that our action is more intentional, wiser, less ego-centered, and more directed toward God's purposes. Prayer enables us to step back and gain perspective on all the busyness that otherwise fills our lives.

The Benedictine tradition has for centuries built this insight into the structure of monastic life. In his famous Rule, a guide for monastic communities, Benedict (ca. 480–547) instructs monks to pause seven times a day for prayer. Leaving aside their work, they were to come together to say the Divine Office or Liturgy of the Hours, a service of Scripture reading, silent prayer, and singing of psalms. The Rule emphasizes the importance of a regular, balanced rhythm of prayer, work, rest, and study in community. The contemporary Benedictine sister Joan Chittister describes her own experience of this way of life:

> It is so easy for good people to confuse their own work with the work of creation. . . . It is so easy to commit ourselves to this century's demand for product and action until the product consumes us and the actions exhaust us and we can no longer remember why we set out to do them in the first place. But regularity in prayer cures all that. Regularity harnesses us to our place in the universe. . . . Benedict called for prayer at regular intervals of each day, right in the middle of apparently urgent and important work. The message is unequivocal. Let no one forget what they are really about.[1]

The "pause" of prayer may be particularly important for people who work passionately for social change. David Stevens is the leader of the Corrymeela Community in Northern Ireland. Corrymeela is an ecumenical Christian community devoted to reconciliation in a country that has seen decades of violent conflict between Protestants and Catholics. Set on the beautiful north Antrim coast, the community seeks to be a reconciling space, opening its doors to groups of all kinds. It is difficult work, dependent on faith and small glimmers of hope amid persistent sectarian fighting. Reflecting on his own long involvement in this effort at reconciliation, Stevens described prayer as a reminder of hope for social activists like himself. He said that social activists tend to be idealistic and thus chronically depressed, because "politics always disappoints." Prayer is an important way to "slow down, connect with the transcendent, and recall that we are simply 'passing through.' It is not all up to me."[2] Prayer, then, is a kind of humble pause in the midst of even terribly important work, putting our human efforts in perspective, helping to sustain the spirit and endurance of those working for social transformation.

PRAYING THE CONFUSION

Prayer, then, is critical in an engaged life. It is also where we meet some of the most difficult spiritual questions. It is when we try to pray that we face head-on our questions about where God is, who we are, how we can come to know God and God's purposes. I was recently gripped by a news story about a carload of seven children—as young as twenty months—all killed in a fiery crash in Florida. A fifteen-year-old was driving. A tractor-trailer behind her smashed into the car, pushing it into a school bus stopped in front of her. The car burst into flames and the five adopted foster children and their two cousins died. On hearing the news, the grandfather of the children collapsed and died of a heart attack. The family was left with loss—total, abrupt, incomprehensible loss. It is a deeply troubling story, perhaps particularly awful to me as I am the mother of small children. I have not found it easy or natural to pray about the situation; in fact I have carefully kept the story at a distance. Why? I suspect that I possess no language to put my feelings into words for prayer, and I am hesitant to ask the big questions that would tumble out if I let them. How could this happen? Where was God in this? How on earth will the families of those children live through the pain?

I could pray for those children. I could pray for some measure of comfort and peace for the family. Yet these prayers seemed to keep a lid on the underlying, heartbreaking question: How could this happen? There are many events posing such questions, even more pressing in situations where suffering results from intentional human action (a husband murders his wife and child, a woman is raped, terrorists commit mass murder). There we are forced to wonder what evil is in human beings. How do we make sense of the awful things that people do to one another?

The gospels clearly invite us to bring our requests to God. The Lord's Prayer is filled with petition ("give us this day our daily bread . . . forgive us our debts . . . rescue us from the evil one"; Matthew 6:9–13). In the gospel of Luke, Jesus teaches the disciples this prayer and then directly tells them a parable about a person roused from sleep in the middle of the night by the persistent knocking of a friend who requests bread. "So I say to you, ask, and it will be given to you; search, and you will find; knock, and the door will be opened for you. For everyone who asks receives, and everyone who searches finds, and for everyone who knocks, the door will be opened" (Luke 11:9–10).

Still, if we pay any attention to what is happening in our world, we may find ourselves wondering whether God does intervene in the course of human action or natural events. Does petitionary prayer make any sense? In fact, many people today, given our extraordinary exposure to events happening across the globe and our science-oriented mind-set, understandably question whether their prayer matters. Does our prayer actually change God's mind, drawing God to act in a way that God would not otherwise act? Or does prayer at least transform us, calm us down, foster compassion, shape our action? These are tough questions.

We also face the problem of discerning God's will, not in generalities but in the particularities of concrete situations. It is one thing to affirm that God desires justice and dignity for all. It is another thing to be specific about what that means in any particular policy debate, be it about foreign policy or stem cell research or abortion. Deciding how faith leads to a certain course of action becomes complicated. Our understanding of the facts of the situation may be incorrect or incomplete. We may not accurately predict the consequences of how we act—what will happen if this person gets elected, or this law gets passed, or this program is put in place. Choices are often messy, with no pure moral option. On top of all this, discernment of what God wills is by its nature a humble, complex process prone to self-deception and the limitations of human knowledge.

I suspect that prayer fully engaged with the social and political events of the world challenges our theology, raising questions we may want to dismiss with easy answers or compartmentalization of spirituality away from the "world." But there in the mix of both conviction and confusion, our prayer is most real and earnest. There is, I think, a place for praying the confusion. The Reformed theologian and pastor Karl Barth, for example, composed this pastoral prayer: "Remain unchanging, O God, both above and in the human actions and events of our days, so confusing and confused, oppressing and oppressive."[3]

This book does not answer those deeply troubling questions about theodicy, about how a loving and all-powerful God can permit evil to persist in the world. Nor does it provide a simple answer to how one discerns God's will. It leads us into those questions as they emerge in real practices and life situations. It shows how some Christians have tried to pray their way into and through those questions, seeking to live faithfully and continue praying amid persistent suffering, injustice, conflict—and, still, hope. In walking with these stories, readers are invited to enter into those same questions in their own lives.

ENTERING INTO THE STORIES

As we enter into these questions, we will try to tease out more specifically what makes integration of prayer and social action complex in practice. Stories of communities in a number of contexts help us look at actual practices of prayer rather than simply discussing the topic as an abstraction:

- A congregational church in Florida erupts in conflict over the outspoken politics of its pastor, opening up a debate about how spirituality and politics should relate in the life of a diverse faith community.

- South Africans try to pray in the face of relentless injustice, and church leaders wind up in a painful controversy about how to pray for political change. At a funeral to bury four anti-apartheid activists, people lift up their voices in grief as they raise their fists in defiant protest against the government; then, as the nation turns to a new future, some turn to prayer as they struggle with the possibility of forgiveness and reconciliation.

- In the dusty fields of California, Cesar Chavez and the Mexican American farm workers he led weave traditional spiritual practices such as fasting, pilgrimage, and celebration of the Eucharist into a savvy campaign for economic justice. The integration draws support but also questions about the line between authentic prayer and political campaigning, and about the place of spiritual practice in an increasingly pluralistic movement.

- When prolife supporters bring their prayer to the streets in the current day, they are sometimes lambasted for hurtful and threatening displays of piety. Prolife and prochoice supporters both pray, but the vast differences in their prayer inevitably push questions of truth while their deep divisions lead us to consider how healing might come to the body.

- Then, from the calm hills of Burgundy, France, the ecumenical Taizé community invites us to be still. Taizé offers another model: prayer itself as the witness and mission, not for the sake of some social aim but as the core of a life of faith. It is a story that, particularly seen alongside the others, brings us to wrestle anew with the relationship between contemplation and action in the Christian life.

I urge readers to step into these stories, to imagine yourselves there in those contexts, and to wrestle with the dilemmas the people faced. The stories are like case studies, deliberately open-ended so that you can live in them and consider how you would have acted, walking in those shoes. In the process, you may bring your own questions to the stories, reflect on your own beliefs about and practices of prayer, and open yourselves to new ways of praying.

I have intentionally chosen some examples that may not be close or familiar to some readers; they are drawn from a number of countries and times. Sometimes we can see things when we step back a little from our own situation. Each story opens questions and insights—about how to keep praying through injustice, how to authentically make our prayer a social witness, how to discern the fine line between presumptuous and prophetic prayer, how to relate contemplation and action, how to pray as a community amid great diversity. We get a glimpse of the power of these people's experience and the depth of their spiritual dilemma.

At points in each of the chapters, I introduce resources from the Judeo-Christian tradition, guidance in the practice of prayer. Chapter Two starts us off by framing our discussion of prayer in dialogue with three streams of the

Christian spiritual tradition: the desert fathers and mothers, Ignatian spirituality, and the mystical writing of Teresa of Avila. Even though volumes have been written on prayer (and I do not attempt any kind of comprehensive overview), these three glimpses into the tradition highlight the centrality of prayer in the Christian way of life and its deep connections to humility, discernment, and action. At the same time, the glimpses reveal the ambiguity of the tradition when it comes to relating spirituality to a life deeply engaged with the world. Too often, prayer has been taught as a practice that requires disengagement from and devaluing of the world. In effect, this book is an invitation to draw deeply from the wells of the Christian spiritual tradition while also creatively engaging—from the perspective of concrete contemporary spiritual dilemmas—those places of silence or misguided counsel.

We may have forgotten, or not known, about some of the wisdom of the Christian tradition when it comes to prayer. In some cases, we have to connect traditional resources and our own contemporary questions, drawing out implications of, for example, Ignatian teaching on discernment for the social and political decisions that we face in our own contexts. Sometimes we need to "speak back" to the tradition and forge another way of appropriating it. I want to emphasize that my discussion of resources is by no means intended to be a quick fix or to pose an easy answer to the dilemma individuals and communities face in integrating prayer and public living. Rather, I aim to bring their practices and those very real dilemmas into dialogue with voices and witnesses within the tradition. I also want to shed light on how their own practices might be relevant to the wider Christian community in differing contexts.

OPENING UP CONVERSATION

My hope is that this book will stimulate conversation, reflection, debate, study, clarification, and renewed practice. Let me emphasize that the book seeks to open up a conversation, not close it down with premature or easy answers. The questions, insights, and practices discussed here need to be considered within varied ecclesial frameworks and social contexts. Christians share a belief that the Bible must guide our discernment about social questions, but we interpret the Bible differently. We also draw upon tradition, reason, and experience in our own ways as sources of truth, illuminating our understanding of the Scriptures. I hope, then, that this book will be a resource that sparks reflection and more faithful practice within the particularities of varied Christian communities and unfolding social situations.

In addition to reflection and conversation, we need models, inspiration, teachers who can lead us to more faithful ways of praying and acting in the world. The communities and individuals that appear on the pages of this book may fill those shoes. We may find ourselves walking with companions who disturb us, inspire us, guide us. We may find ourselves opening up to new ways of praying. Certainly, one does not learn to pray simply by reading a book. Prayer is an encounter, a relationship that is eminently personal and unique to each individual. We learn to pray by praying; there is a great deal of truth in that. Yet we can also find ourselves blocked or stuck. We do not know how to pray. Or we pray in ways that only reinforce false and damaging understanding of God. Here is where we can benefit from guides that show us another path. We also benefit simply from recalling that we are part of a wider community that is seeking to be faithful. We may differ in what that means, but together we gain from wrestling within the community.

Chapter 2

A CLOUD OF WITNESSES: PRAYER AND THE CHRISTIAN WAY OF LIFE

——

One of the fourth-century desert fathers, Abba Macarius, was asked "How should one pray?" The old man said, "There is no need at all to make long discourses; it is enough to stretch out one's hands and say, 'Lord, as you will, and as you know, have mercy.'"

Macarius was among the early monks and nuns who led solitary lives in the deserts of Egypt, Palestine, and Syria. They left cities and towns to live a stark, ascetic life of prayer, confronting the demons within and without, seeking to grow in discernment and purity of heart. People often came to them and asked for a "word"—

for spiritual counsel. The elders would respond with short sayings directed to the person, getting right to the heart of his or her struggle or vice.

Macarius left his village to go to the desert of Scetis in Egypt, where he lived in a cell and traveled around the desert to see other monks. His experience of long hours in prayer flows into the word that he offers to others. Macarius emphasizes the trust and humility integral to prayer. Prayer means opening oneself to the will of God, abandoning oneself to it, and clinging always to the promise of God's mercy. The desert elder did not underestimate the depth of struggle human beings experience in their lives; he goes on to counsel: "And if the conflict grows fiercer, say, 'Lord, help!'" But then, Macarius says, still trust: "He [God] knows very well what we need and he shews us his mercy."[1] The abba was not offering a simplistic salve but rather articulating the few, trusting, humble words that are necessary in prayer.

For the desert elders, prayer was a way of life. They sought to live into the apostle Paul's counsel to "pray without ceasing." According to John Cassian, whose *Conferences* depict conversations with monks of the Egyptian desert, Abba Isaac told him, "Whoever is in the habit of praying only at the hour when the knees are bent prays very little."[2] Constant prayer paves the way for the perfection of one's heart; at the same time, purity of heart and the enlightenment of the Holy Spirit enable the person to pray well. It is a theme that resounds for centuries in Eastern Orthodox spirituality. Ceaseless repetition of the "Jesus Prayer" ("Lord, Jesus Christ, have mercy on me") purifies the heart and leads to inner freedom and stillness. As the

LORD, HAVE MERCY

Russian peasant describes in the anonymous nineteenth-century classic *The Way of a Pilgrim,* this humble prayer, an "abbreviated form of the gospel," can eventually flow from a person as naturally as breath.[3]

The desert elders looked to the psalms as a basis of unceasing prayer. Every day at dusk and again in the middle of the night, they individually prayed the divine office, which included reciting twelve psalms, and they meditated on the psalms throughout the day while they did their manual labor. On Sundays, they gathered for communal prayer—again, heavily emphasizing the chanting of psalms—and for Eucharist.[4] According to Cassian, Abba Isaac counsels monks to meditate constantly on a line from Psalm 70: "O God, incline unto my aid; O Lord, make haste to help me" (Psalm 70:1, as quoted by Cassian). The prayer "contains an invocation of God in the face of any crisis, the humility of a devout confession, the watchfulness of concern and of constant fear, a consciousness of one's own frailty, the assurance of being heard, and confidence in a protection that is always present." Repeating this prayer in all circumstances brings a "perpetual awareness of God."[5]

Although their vision was for prayer to be constant, woven seamlessly into every moment of the day, prayer was not necessarily easy for these desert monks and nuns. They believed they were engaged in a real battle for the soul; demons would tempt them—often to the sin of pride—as Satan tempted Jesus in the desert (Matthew 4:1–11). Demons would deceive them about themselves and lure them to false attachments. Thus Abba Agathon could say: "I think there is no labour greater than that of prayer to

God. For every time a man wants to pray, his enemies, the demons, want to prevent him, for they know that it is only by turning him from prayer that they can hinder his journey. . . . Prayer is warfare to the last breath."[6]

The desert elders offer a startling witness to the urgency and centrality of prayer. Their message on the relationship between prayer and action in the world is, perhaps, more ambiguous. After all, they did leave cities and towns to live in remote areas, some as hermits in tiny cells, miles away from the centers of power of the Roman Empire. Some monks were known for spectacular feats of asceticism and extreme solitude. Symeon Stylite avoided visitors to his monastery, for example, by climbing atop a pillar and living there in prayer for more than thirty years. It is difficult in such a case to see how prayer is deeply engaged with the realities and sufferings of the world. The sayings of the desert fathers often counsel strict detachment from the things of this world as necessary for intense relationship with God.

Yet some would see in their desert withdrawal not a retreat from the world but rather an alternative, starkly countercultural witness to that world, in which they saw Christianity accommodating to the culture and mores of the Roman Empire. Moreover, in most of the desert elders' sayings and lives prayer certainly is not detached from compassion. Hospitality is a key practice for those who live in the desert. In their spiritual counsel, the desert elders carefully connect prayer, humility, self-examination, and deep compassion for human frailty.

The sixth-century monk Dorotheos of Gaza offered this word: "Suppose we were to take a compass and insert the point and draw the outline of the circle. . . . Let us suppose that this circle is the world and that God is the center." As human beings draw closer to God, moving from the outer edge of the circle to the center, they also draw closer to one another. "The closer they are to God, the closer they become to one another; and the closer they are to one another, the closer they become to God," noted Dorotheos. As contemporary theologian Roberta Bondi explains in reflecting on this saying, the monk teaches that intimacy with God cannot be separated from love of neighbor; the two go hand in hand. Similarly, as one becomes more distant from the neighbor, one drops back away from the center. Prayer and love of neighbor are intimately linked.[7] Thus the scholar of early monasticism Douglas Burton-Christie describes a rhythm of "withdrawal, encounter, and return." Periods of withdrawal for intense prayer and self-examination are important for the spiritual life, but they are not an end in themselves; rather, they flow back into community.[8]

LIVING GENEROUSLY: IGNATIUS OF LOYOLA

The Spanish soldier and founder of the Jesuit order Ignatius of Loyola (1491–1556) lived in a very different time and place. Yet he too came to an understanding of prayer as central to the Christian life. In many ways, Ignatius lived quite opposite to the way the desert ascetics did. The early monks and nuns retreated to the desert;

Ignatius brought his mission to the cities—to Barcelona and Rome, to Jerusalem and Paris. Many desert elders lived in solitude; Ignatius traveled with a band of companions, fellow visionaries and missionaries, who would become the "Society of Jesus" or the Jesuits. They would work actively to serve the church in a tumultuous time—a time of massive ecclesial corruption and the challenge of the Reformation—through evangelization, education, and spiritual guidance. Like the desert ascetics, though, Ignatius left behind a witness to the importance of prayer, humility, and discernment. For Ignatius, prayer guided one to perceive one's purpose in life, make right choices, and act generously in the world.

Ignatius of Loyola led a carefree, nobleman's life until about the age of twenty, when he was wounded in a battle against the French in Pamplona. As he spent long months recuperating from a serious leg injury, he began to reflect on his life, which he would later describe as "given to the vanities of the world."[9] During this time of slow recovery and immobility, he did not have access to the books of chivalry he enjoyed and instead was given a copy of the *Life of Christ* and a book about the saints. He began to feel torn, alternately absorbed in his usual worldly fantasies and drawn by a new desire to live as the saints did, in service of God. Gradually he noticed that although he took a surface delight in thinking about resuming his former life, indulging in chivalrous fantasies, those thoughts eventually left him feeling tired and dry. On the other hand, when he contemplated going on pilgrimage to Jerusalem and following the saints in an ascetic life, those thoughts left him feeling joyful. This was the beginning of what he came to describe as the "discernment of spirits." Ignatius believed that as we make decisions and choices, careful attention to abiding feelings of "consolation" and "desolation" point us to what is of God and what is not of God. Consolation is a deep feeling of rightness, joy, and peacefulness. Desolation, on the other hand, is marked by feelings of anxiety, disorder, despair, and turmoil. Ignatius started paying attention to these deeper feelings, which he believed were prompted by good or evil spirits. He decided to make a major change in his life.

Once he was well, he set out on a pilgrimage to Jerusalem. He stopped along the way in the Spanish mountain town of Montserrat, where he exchanged his fine clothes for beggar's sackcloth and laid down his arms before a statue of the Virgin Mary in an all-night prayer vigil. He continued to the town of Manresa, where he expected to stay only a few days. He ended up remaining for nearly a year, living a hermit's life in a cave, praying deeply, experiencing mystical gifts, and drafting what became known as "The Spiritual Exercises." The Exercises were intended to guide others in serious, prayerful reflection on their lives, helping them to enter imaginatively into Scripture and offer themselves to God in a generous and free act of decision. Ignatius saw his work as a kind of guide to retreat leaders who could use the Exercises flexibly to help others grow in their faith and make major choices about their purpose in life, their vocation. Ignatius and his companions gave the Exercises to many people; their own discernment process led them to go before Pope Paul III to offer themselves as a new order in service to the church. The art of discerning the spirits was central to the Exercises, which continues to serve as a popular retreat guide for spiritual seekers today.

Ignatius found it essential to cut through dispersion of our thoughts and inclinations, to focus our choices on our ultimate purpose in life. Thus, he writes in "The Spiritual Exercises": "The eye of our intention ought to be single. I ought to focus only on the purpose for which I was created, to praise God and to save my soul." Everything we choose should be chosen to further that end. This is the "principle and foundation" of all discernment. Ignatius was keenly aware of how we deceive ourselves, allowing our own desires to rule, telling ourselves that what we want must be what God wants. Pause, he says, step back: "I should find myself in the middle, like the pointer of a balance, in order to be ready to follow that which I perceive to be more to the glory and praise of God our Lord and the salvation of my soul."[10] Ignatian spirituality invites us to use our reason, imagination, prayer, and reflection on Scripture to determine how best to use the goods of creation in furthering the end for which we are created. The idea of doing "all for the greater glory of God" continues as the Jesuit motto and guide for communal and individual discernment today.

To aid in our growth as persons of freedom and discernment, Ignatius also strongly encouraged a daily "examen," or what has been described as an examination of consciousness. This practice is a kind of daily checkup, a time of prayer and reflection on the day, where we ask God to help us to know our failings and take an "account of my soul."[11] Contemporary writers have suggested that

LORD, HAVE MERCY

one ask of oneself two questions every day—such as "Where have I been most loving today? Where was I least loving today?"[12] Over time, one comes to see patterns—which activities and relationships draw one closer to God, which leave one feeling dispersed and decentered. With prayer, one gains the freedom to choose those things that draw one closer to God and say no to the others. The examen, then, is an aid to discernment.

Ignatius understood discernment as a process, a practice honed over a lifetime. His deliberations were marked by both uncertainty and points of clarity, with resolutions offered up humbly in prayer: "When that election or decision has been made, the person who has made it ought with great diligence to go to prayer before God our Lord, to offer him that election, and to beg his Divine Majesty to receive and confirm it, provided it is conducive to his greater service and praise."[13] Ignatius believed that one can find God in all things and that prayerful discernment must be woven into all kinds of action. Ignatian spirituality does not offer certainty, but rather a way of living into the questions prayerfully and attentively.

PRAYER AS FRIENDSHIP:
TERESA OF AVILA

Another Spanish spiritual guide, Teresa of Avila (1515–1582), a mystic and preeminent teacher on prayer, described prayer as "nothing else than an intimate sharing between friends."[14] Teresa knew about friendship and about prayer;

she was sociable and as a teenager quite absorbed in what she later would see as vain friendships. Inspired by spiritual books and conversation, she made a decision at age twenty (against her father's wishes) to enter a nearby Carmelite monastery and live as a nun. She experienced terrible health problems and great difficulty in prayer for years before experiencing the intense mystical encounters in prayer for which she has become famous. She remains a teacher of prayer who knows its difficulties and all the more so extols its importance. Prayer, she wrote, means frequently taking time to be alone with the One who we know loves us. We open our hearts to God and seek for our lives to be aligned with God's purposes for us. Though we often think of prayer as words, Teresa's perspective reminds us that fundamentally prayer is relationship. Prayer is, in her words, "an exercise of love."[15]

As in any relationship, there can be periods of difficulty and dryness. We may know Teresa as a saint and doctor of the church, but in her autobiography she describes feeling distracted, caught up in vain pastimes, absorbed by relationships that dragged her down. At one point, she stopped praying for more than a year. That was a grave mistake, she writes, for "in this life there could be no greater good than the practice of prayer."[16]

Teresa was acutely aware of her own weakness. Prayer depended, in her experience, on humility and openness to God's great grace. She describes the importance of aligning her will with that of God: "In order that love be true and the friendship endure, the wills of the friends must be in accord."[17] Discernment is a critical part of the life of prayer. Teresa believed, as did many others of her time, that the devil leads us astray. The devil may delude us such that we interpret our experience wrongly. The devil may distract us, puff us up, cause us to stop praying, seduce us into ungodly relationships and habits. Only with discernment in prayer can we perceive what is truly of God and grow in true humility. Teresa, like Ignatius, found a way to recognize what is of God partly through careful attention to her interior states. The devil is recognized clearly by the disquiet and affliction it brings to the soul. "True humility," on the other hand, "doesn't come to the soul with agitation or disturbance, nor does it darken it or bring it dryness. Rather, true humility consoles and acts in a completely opposite way: quietly, gently, and with light. . . . His [the Lord's] mercy lifts its spirits."[18]

Although she attends closely to her own experience in prayer, for Teresa it would be unthinkable to discern and pray outside the community of the church. She repeatedly discusses her experience with confessors, testing her experience against the wisdom of the church. She does not always agree with her confessors, and she finds ways to defend the authority of her own experience of God. This is a bold move, because she is writing during the Inquisition—a dangerous time for anyone whose experience might be judged as outside the bounds of orthodoxy. Hers is a delicate dance, sharing her extraordinary experiences of God while not stepping on the toes of the church. Yet the church is her dance partner; her prayer is rooted in the life and teachings of the community.

Teresa receives abundant experience of mystical grace, like God saturating the garden of her soul with plentiful rain. As God draws her more and more deeply to prayer, she finds that God does the work in her while she rests joyfully in God. She even describes a kind of union with God, a "joining with heavenly love."[19] Those experiences can lead her to devalue the world and even her own life: "From this prayer comes the pain of having to return to everyday life."[20] This is unfortunately a real and common theme in the Christian spiritual tradition; holiness is often understood as requiring or producing extreme detachment from worldly pursuits, relationships, and concerns.

Still, Teresa did come down from the heights of mystical rapture to straddle a horse and ride tirelessly around Spain establishing a new structure of religious life, a more rigorous Carmelite order. She was distressed at how lax the nuns had become in her convent, and she set out to reform the order. Navigating ecclesial and local politics, she gained approval for new convents and monasteries throughout Spain. Teresa was, in fact, transforming structures, envisioning and building new organizations. She can speak of being oblivious to everything but her longing for God, but she also writes that "God can be served in everything."[21]

THE POWER AND THE AMBIGUITY

What these stories of the desert elders, Ignatius, and Teresa show is a common thread of the tradition: the centrality of prayer to the Christian way of life. The practice

LORD, HAVE MERCY

of prayer actually is the path to knowledge of God; prayer is part of the faith that seeks understanding. This understanding of prayer has unfortunately been undermined by a false separation of spirituality from theology that began in the high Middle Ages and continues today, leaving devotion privatized and disconnected from a whole life that seeks wisdom. For the desert elders, Ignatius, and Teresa, the practice of prayer was integral to a way of life that seeks true understanding of God and self.

These voices also witness to the importance of humility and discernment in a prayerful life. Ignatius and Teresa experience a kind of conversion that entails turning away from vain ambition and prideful delights. They constantly test their experience, watching for self-deception and error. In the face of God's great grace, they are drawn to careful meditation on their own sinfulness. So too do the desert elders stand guard against the very human temptation to pride and self-deception, the tendency to substitute our will for God's and forget to pray for God's mercy. According to Cassian, Abba Isaac puts it clearly: "So that prayer may be made with the fervor and purity that it deserves. . . . the unshakeable foundations of deep humility should be laid, which can support a tower that will penetrate the heavens."[22]

The streams of tradition show too that although solitude can deeply nourish prayer, Christian prayer is not private in the sense of being disconnected from a community. Even the desert solitaries gathered for communal prayer in the liturgical tradition of the church. Christian prayer takes place in a web of relationships and ultimately is rooted in the life of the church. For Ignatius, this entails

A Cloud of Witnesses

absolute agreement with the teachings of the church. Others, such as Teresa of Avila, stand more precariously on the margins of the church, but still deeply woven into its fabric.

At the same time, these ancestors in the faith also sometimes reveal an unfortunate devaluing of the world that works its way into many spiritual writings in the Christian heritage. In part, this is a contemporary misunderstanding of the meaning of detachment. Many spiritual writers underscore the importance of stepping back from our relationships and everyday pursuits so as to make sure that our desires are properly ordered. This need not be a rejection of ordinary life but instead a way of gaining perspective, checking our tendency to rush into our own plans, and remembering that ultimately all of life is under God. However, the tradition too often describes prayer and holiness as a gift that takes one out of the world, directing one's love exclusively to God rather than the world, as if it were an either-or. This is, I would say, a false understanding of God's relationship to creation and of the human vocation. The ambiguity of the tradition around the relationship between prayer and life in the world adds to contemporary confusion about spirituality, and this legacy has left us with enduring understandings about how we may practice our faith.

Yet when we look carefully at the tradition, we do find great contemplatives who show that the life of prayer can lead to compassionate and visionary action in the world. Action frequently takes the form of acts of charity (Francis of Assisi caring for the poor, Catherine of Siena tending to the sick). The connection between prayer and works of mercy is well established in the tradition. Less noticed, less explored, is the connection between prayer and action for social change, particularly such as we would confront in a contemporary political context.[23] How might prayer flow from, ground, or shape a prayerful engagement with complex social, political, and economic situations? We move forward now to explore just such dilemmas in their concreteness, keeping our eye on how the tradition may be brought creatively into the dialogue.

Chapter 3

SPIRITUALITY AND POLITICS: TENSIONS WITHIN A CONGREGATION

———

Coral Gables Congregational Church (CGCC) stands directly across from the towers of the luxurious Biltmore Hotel in a small, wealthy city just on the outskirts of Miami. In a neighborhood of well-groomed homes in Spanish-style architecture, the church is an historic site as the oldest church in Coral Gables. It seems a protected space, calm, even pampered. Yet things in this congregation are far from settled. For several years now, church members have been engaged in an energetic and painful debate about its identity and mission. There are many layers to the tension: internal politics and personality conflict, turf issues, discomfort with open communication, money, and diversity. The church members are also raising questions that will sound familiar to other faith communities: What does it mean to be "spiritual"? Should spirituality and politics mix, and if so, whose politics should prevail? How do we bring faith and politics together in a diverse congregation?

From its origins in 1923, CGCC set out to sound a progressive note in the relatively conservative political and religious climate of south Florida. Theologically liberal, the congregation prides itself on being a diverse, inclusive, and socially active community. The congregation has identified itself as "open and affirming," a hospitable space for gay, lesbian, bisexual, and transgender persons. Supported by a vote of its members, ministers perform homosexual unions. Like its surrounding community of Coral Gables, the congregation is wealthy, highly educated, and predominantly white.[1] Its membership contrasts with the far more heavily Latino and poorer population of the city of Miami. Still, the members, numbering about six hundred, are not homogeneous in their political views. Recent members drawn from the Catholic and Baptist churches that dominate the religious scene in south Florida carry with them more conservative social and political positions, as do many younger Cuban Americans, who are overwhelmingly Republican. Some of the oldest members of the church resist mixing politics and prayer; one gentleman who has been a member for fifty years says simply: "Keep politics out of the sanctuary." As a result, the congregation holds a mix of age, political affiliations, faith backgrounds, and assumptions about what it means to be spiritual and to be church. How, then, do they live and pray together as a Christian community?

A Pastor Stirs the Water

Donna Schaper believes passionately in working for social justice. As a college student in the late 1960s, she was active in the civil rights movement and in opposing the Vietnam War. After college she went to divinity school and became an ordained minister in the United Church of Christ. As a female minister in the early 1970s, she was used to breaking through barriers. She was repeatedly the first woman pastor to fill positions—as a chaplain at Yale University working under William Sloane Coffin, and as pastor of local churches in Amherst, Massachusetts, and on Long Island, New York. She took on leadership roles within the United Church of Christ, overseeing more than a hundred churches in western Massachusetts. Schaper was politically active, outspoken, and prolific. She wrote books on the practice of Sabbath and on gardening. Married to a Jewish man and the mother of three children, she published a book on inter-faith parenting.

After many years of ministry in New England, Schaper made a big move. She accepted the position of senior pastor at Coral Gables Congregational Church; it was the first time a woman had ever assumed that position in the congregation. She wasted no time in getting her vision out on the table. Soon after she arrived, for example, she wrote a letter to the editor of the *Miami Herald* calling for a state income tax, much to the chagrin of some church members. It was not long before tensions surfaced within the congregation.

Three Vignettes

Three vignettes offer a glimpse into these tensions and the deeper issues of spirituality, politics, and church that lie just below the surface.

Free Trade

It was the fall of 2003. Miami was preparing to host the Free Trade Agreement of the Americas (FTAA) Conference, a gathering of international business and political leaders to move forward plans for a free trade agreement across North, Central, and South America. The FTAA was highly controversial, like its predecessor, the North American Free Trade Agreement (NAFTA), initiated in 1994. Proponents saw it as an opportunity to reduce barriers to trade between the United States and Latin America and to stimulate the economies of member countries. Critics, however, objected that the agreement would increase poverty and hurt workers.

Several months before the FTAA gathering, Pastor Schaper received a request from the national United Church of Christ Justice and Witness Ministries, asking that Coral Gables Congregational Church host a group of visitors coming to Miami for the FTAA event to express their views to the "powers that be." Schaper and a task force of church members agreed. They planned to let the visitors sleep in the church fellowship hall. The decision sparked outrage among some church members and drew suspicion upon the church from law enforcement agencies.

The City of Miami was determined to keep control during the conference. Police prepared for massive demonstrations and put plans in place to contain protests. They readied hundreds of riot police. They feared the force of "anarchists" and resolved to prevent interruption of the FTAA meetings or damage to property and persons. They gave little attention to how to protect the rights of demonstrators (some of whom would describe Miami as a "police state" that week in November). An Independent Review Panel would later condemn excessive use of force by the Miami police against nonviolent protesters and its trampling of civil rights. The "overwhelming riot-clad police presence, when there was no civil disturbance, chilled citizen participation in permitted and lawful demonstrations and events," concluded the panel.[2]

In this highly charged atmosphere, the Coral Gables assistant chief of police visited the church and, according to Schaper and a leader of the congregation's Justice and Peace Committee, Roy Wasson, noted his own view that churches should stick to matters of religious doctrine and keep out of social issues. He encouraged the congregation to reconsider its plan to house protesters. The Coral Gables city manager told the church that it could not host visitors without breaking local building and zoning laws.[3] Church members became concerned about the plan to host the visitors; some were quite angry at the pastor. The plan was scrapped, though some church members individually hosted a small group of visitors in their private homes. Instead, the congregation sponsored an Open Forum about the FTAA during the week of the conference.

Apparently, police kept a close eye on the church nevertheless, tracking its activities. Official police documents described the pastor as "very anti-FTAA" and included the Open Forum on a list of anti-FTAA activities across Miami. The pastor and the Justice and Peace Committee strongly objected to what they saw as highly inappropriate state interference with the activities of their church. They also described divisions that arose within the congregation in this pressured environment:

> Apart from the suggestion of criminality from the fact of investigation, the label of "very anti-FTAA" surely drove (or drove more deeply) a wedge between some attendees of the Church . . . just based on the politics of such things. The church has members who were troubled by having a pastor who is branded as an anti-establishment sort of person. Members stayed home some Sundays and others quit over the perceived "political" position of the pastor. Similarly, at least some non-members in search of a church home might be less likely to visit because the local authorities have branded the church as "bad for business."[4]

If Schaper picked up the conflict within the congregation, she nevertheless did not mince words in her sermon that week. From the pulpit the Sunday after the FTAA meetings, she sharply condemned the city's actions. A visitor stood up and interrupted her sermon to assert his support for George W. Bush. Members describe that Sunday as a low point of worship at Coral Gables.

The publicity did have an impact. The congregation drew praise from one liberal group, the People for the

LORD, HAVE MERCY

American Way, an organization that describes itself as battling the influence of the radical right. They awarded Rev. Schaper and the congregation a Free Speech Award for providing a forum for debate during the FTAA meeting.[5] One church member who joined the church shortly after the FTAA events said that, to this day, a neighbor still asks her why on earth she goes to that "way-out church."

Prayer and a Boycott

Coral Gables lies within miles of acres and acres of fields worked by migrant farm workers. Rows of tomatoes, strawberries, and lettuce grow under the hot sun. The workers pick the crops for minimal pay, with no benefits or legal protections. Many are undocumented immigrants from Mexico. The farm workers are vital to south Florida's agricultural economy, but they are among the poorest of the poor.

Flush with money as stock within their endowment went public, CGCC decided to make a substantial commitment to better the situation of the farm workers. In 2002 they agreed to fund a staff person to open a Miami office of the National Farm Worker Ministry, an interfaith organization that supports farm workers' struggle for justice. The congregation's Justice and Peace Committee made the farm workers an important priority. They sought to educate the larger congregation about the plight of the farm workers and to engage their fellow church members in activism and prayer on the farm workers' behalf.

A Florida farm worker organization, the Coalition of Immokalee Workers or CIW, had called for a boycott against Taco Bell, one of the largest purchasers of toma-toes from south Florida. According to the CIW, tomato pickers earned a median annual income of only about $7,500. The organization sought a raise in wages and argued that Taco Bell had the economic resources to pay the tomato growers more, which in turn would result in higher wages for the workers. They also demanded that Taco Bell take leadership to improve labor relations and better working conditions for the tomato pickers.[6]

The Justice and Peace Committee of the church backed the boycott. They participated in rallies outside Taco Bell franchises in the Miami area. They organized a candlelight prayer vigil to remember fasting farm work-ers who were protesting against Taco Bell. They prayed, then, not simply for a general cause—justice for farm workers—but more specifically in support of a strategy to accomplish that justice: the boycott against Taco Bell. Is this level of specificity in prayer problematic, or an appro-priate stand on the side of justice?

The Justice and Peace Committee members clearly thought it was a faithful stance. They encouraged church members (once during Sunday worship) to boycott. This infuriated some business leaders within the congregation, including one of the church's top donors. They saw their church going "antibusiness" and politics taking over the service.

For those within the church who supported the boy-cott, though, this action was a natural implication of their faith. They were called to practice justice. Biblical texts shaped or at least confirmed their sense of calling. The Justice and Peace Committee points on its informational flyers, for example, to this passage from the prophet Isaiah: "How terrible it will be for those who make unfair laws, and those who write laws that make life hard for people. They are not fair to the poor and they rob my people of their rights" (Isaiah 10:1–2, as cited by Justice and Peace Committee), and to this text from the gospel of Matthew: " 'Truly, I tell you, just as you did it to one of the least of these who are members of my family, you did it to me' " (Matthew 25:40).

The committee also looks to national United Church of Christ statements to support its mission. Indeed, the general synod of the UCC denomination had endorsed the boycott in the summer of 2001, urging "all settings of the United Church of Christ to boycott Taco Bell until it practices corporate responsibility by demanding a living wage for the Immokalee workers."[7] The synod saw the boycott as a Christian practice, a way to integrate faith with economic actions and speak for those who are powerless: "Being Christian disciples implies that the values of our faith must inform all aspects of our lives—including our purchasing and investment choices. . . . The United Church of Christ strives to be an important witness in the global marketplace. Since farm workers are denied the right to organize and engage in collective bargaining, we must speak for those who are denied voice."[8] Other Christian churches took a similar stance. The Presbyterian Church (USA) endorsed the boycott in June 2002 and the General Conference of the United Methodist Church joined the boycott in May 2004. The National Council of Churches endorsed the boycott in 2003, the first one the organization supported since its

1988 boycott of Royal Dutch/Shell operating in apartheid South Africa.[9]

However, within UCC polity, statements of the denominational offices do not have authority in the sense that they do in many other traditions. Authority rests in the assembly of each congregation, not in denominational statements, or in the pastor, or in any one church committee. The members discern together who they are and how they should practice their faith. Who, then, speaks for the church? Who defines the identity and mission of the congregation?

God Speaks from a Billboard

The billboards appeared around Miami in the winter of 2002, as the United States poised for war with Iraq. "Blessed Are the Peacemakers" read one, echoing Jesus' words in the Sermon on the Mount. "Let There Be Peace on Earth, and Let It Begin with Me," read another. The most strongly worded: "War? Not in my name. Not now. Not ever.—God." The Justice and Peace Committee of Coral Gables Congregational Church paid for two of the billboards. Concerned that the last one would be more controversial, Noel Cleland, one of the committee leaders, used money from a memorial fund for his father, administered by the church. Cleland said: "There is a sense of urgency to do something now. . . . Now it's more important we stand our moral ground."[10] Still, some in the church objected to what seemed a public statement paid for by the congregation, spoken in their name, without their agreement.

National UCC leaders strongly opposed the war in Iraq, arguing that preemptive action would not reduce the threat of terrorism and would only inflict massive human suffering, but at Coral Gables opinions were divided.[11] The Justice and Peace Committee drafted a resolution that opposed an American first-strike attack on Iraq without United Nations sanction. They brought it before the church council, which voted it down. Cleland recalls: "A milder resolution was then approved by the council to avoid having to add to the discomfort that some members felt in trying to deal with this issue. . . . It was a tricky process that added divisiveness to the church."[12]

TENSIONS RISE: WHAT DOES IT MEAN TO BE SPIRITUAL?

Tension within CGCC was rising. A group of members were quite unhappy with the pastor, objecting to politics in the pulpit. They did not want a liberal position forced on them. Some felt the church was losing its identity, becoming overly political, neglecting pastoral care and spiritual nurture. Debate about how to spend the endowment money fed into the conflict. Should the church use it on outreach or inreach? Should the funds go to social justice ministries, or building renovations, or worship and arts programs? Should they dip into the capital of the endowment to make generous donations, or live more strictly within the bounds of the endowment income? At the center of the debate were questions about what it meant to be church and what it meant to be "spiritual." One member had remarked several years earlier that the CGCC budget was that of an "international charitable organization or a university"; he feared that CGCC was "losing its identity and tradition."[13]

In January 2003, some members of the congregation signed a petition that listed grievances about the direction of the congregation and its leadership. The first one: "We do not feel that we are experiencing the spiritual fulfillment that we seek. We are concerned that political and social issues rather than spiritual have taken over as the most important aspect of the service."

Pastor Schaper, however, rejected a dichotomy between the political and the spiritual. She considered it her life mission to provide "spiritual nurture for public capacity."[14] In a response to the petition, she stated: "Were I to do only spiritual nurture, I would find that unbiblical. Were I to do only public capacity building, I would consider that unbiblical. I try to do both and have often said that my goal in preaching is to spiritually strengthen and mature us for our life and work in the world."[15] Rev. Schaper found inspiration in such biblical texts as Micah 6:8 ("What does the Lord require of you, but to do justice, and to love kindness, and to walk humbly with your God?").

What, then, does it mean to be spiritual? Petition signers clearly saw the spiritual as something distinct from politics. They wanted some kind of soul nurture that they did not feel they were getting. Mary Eaton, the church membership director, perceived the situation this way: "Some people joined the church because they were broken, tired, stressed. They needed a word to get them through the week; they did not want the church to push them to another set of demands and action."[16]

Liberation Spirituality: A Latin American Perspective

Should spirituality be a kind of respite from activity and pressure, a way for individuals to heal and to relieve stress? Or should prayer and the life of the church be more integrally related to political action—demanding even a costly engagement? For some Christians, these are urgent questions of survival; they simply cannot afford to divorce their faith from the political and economic issues that affect the survival of their community. Liberation theologians writing from situations of oppression and civil war in Latin America, for example, describe prayer as an integral dimension of the struggle for liberation. Referring to the work of Brazilian theologian Leonardo Boff, a priest serving in Bolivia noted: "The real synthesis is not in prayer *and* action, or action *and* prayer, but prayer *in* action, prayer *in* the struggle for liberation."[17] For Latin American liberation theologians, spirituality cannot be divorced from politics; liberation requires concrete transformation of social structures that bring massive poverty and human rights abuse. These writers caution against a spirituality that is not rooted in the work of justice demanded by particular historical contexts; Christian faith must be embodied in the concrete praxis of liberation for the poor and oppressed. It often involves great cost, living as Jesus lived, prepared to suffer as Jesus suffered on the cross.

Jon Sobrino, a Jesuit teaching in El Salvador, experienced civil war and military dictatorship in that country.

He wrote movingly about those who had endured the ultimate cost—martyrdom at the hands of the state. Sobrino lived through the murder of the Salvadoran archbishop Oscar Romero, an outspoken advocate for human rights and the poor. Government assassins shot Romero dead while he was saying Mass in 1980. That same year, military assassins abducted and murdered three American nuns and a lay missionary working in El Salvador. Then, in 1989, government forces killed six Jesuits and their two female housekeepers in the community residence at the University of Central America, where Sobrino also lived. He happened to be away in Thailand at the time; thus he lived.

Out of experiences such as these and witnessing to the deaths of countless Salvadorans, he wrote about what it means to be a real Christian. Sobrino sharply condemned what he called a "false" spirituality: "I must confess that the word 'spirituality' makes me uncomfortable and even scares me somewhat. The reason for this is that spirituality comes from Spirit, and the Spirit is something that is not visible and is often contrasted with what is material and historical. For this reason, to speak of spirituality can and often does carry us, one way or another, off to an invisible world, or even to an unreal one."[18] For Sobrino, as for other liberation theologians, true Christian spirituality is eminently real, fully in solidarity with the suffering, incarnational as Jesus was flesh among us. Sobrino perceives a deep integration between Christian spirituality and politics (understood as action to transform unjust structures on behalf of the poor and oppressed), such that he can talk of "political holiness."

Looking at the history of Christian spirituality, Sobrino notes that an exclusive focus on the contemplative life has diverted attention from action, wrongly justifying passivity. For Sobrino and other liberation theologians, political action is not something outside of the experience of God, something to which prayer leads if a person gives it enough thought. Rather, action on behalf of the poor and prayer are deeply interrelated encounters with God. In discussing the vision of Peruvian theologian Gustavo Gutiérrez, Sobrino develops this idea:

> The historical reality of the poor is something that not only ought to be analyzed and responded to in accordance with its materiality, but ought to be the object of a spiritual experience, a reality that can "implode" into our lives and so become a mediation of the experience of God. On the other hand, the spiritual experience of encountering God, or of being encountered by God, includes, in virtue of its own dynamic, and not only as a heterogeneous conclusion of a process of ratiocination, the act of going forth to meet historical poverty and applying a remedy.[19]

To separate prayer and politics, then, is not faithful to the Christian call. An exclusive focus on one's interior life, on the inner self, cannot be authentic spirituality. Yet neither can politics be divorced from prayer. Sobrino cautions about collapsing all of spirituality into action: "On the other hand the absolutization of action is not infrequent today either. . . . For those who want their action to be Christian, it is also urgent that they find the correct relationship between action and prayer."[20]

Conflict often arises, though, as political action and analysis takes specific form. The Catholic hierarchy, for example, sharply criticized Latin American liberation theologians for uncritically borrowing from Marxist political ideology. They agreed that the gospel calls on Christians to make a "preferential option for the poor." But what this means in political practice—how to practically achieve relief for the poor—was debated. Similarly, some in Coral Gables resisted Rev. Schaper's particular liberal positions on issues of taxes, war, and trade.

It is certainly true that when it comes to questions of facts and public policy, people of faith and good will can differ. The inevitable conflicts and messiness of politics, the very real possibility of what sociologist Max Weber called "unintended consequences," lead some to resist too closely merging politics and their spiritual life. Perhaps this is one reason the Catholic hierarchy critiqued liberation theologians for "radical politicization of faith's affirmations."[21] Is Christian spirituality somehow about connecting with and resting in a more transcendent, universal, and timeless reality, beyond the compromises, uncertainties, and abuses of politics? Can it be this even though Christian faith is deeply historical and incarnational?

POLITICS IN THE SANCTUARY

At Coral Gables Congregational Church, worship tried to straddle the two visions, often uncomfortably. Pastor Schaper's preaching tended to hit on specific political issues, in partisan tones, riling some in the congregation. One church member who signed the petition commented: "My own opinion was that attendance was declining because she [the pastor] was advocating issues from the pulpit and in writings that were controversial—issues that had another point of view. Also, she did not explain her reasons for advocacy of these issues. I felt that attendance was declining because people did not want to hear her advocacy for so many controversial issues."[22]

The pastoral prayers, on the other hand, tended to lift up social justice issues in more general language, avoiding offense. Beverly Ross, a member who is also ordained and formerly was on staff at the church, composed many pastoral prayers for Sunday worship. Acknowledging Veterans Day 2004, for example, she did not name any particular conflict. She prayed for all government leaders, those in the majority party and in the minority. She prayed for all soldiers and civilian workers as well as all whose towns have been invaded by war. The prayer voiced a longing for peace and an end to violence without naming a specific course of action: "Touch with your Spirit all those who have choices to make about war and in war, that they may yearn and work for peace and wholeness in your world."[23] Ross believes that it is "simply good theology" to weave social justice concerns into prayer. In doing so, she "asks God to speak to our hearts, to help us to act ... prays for a spirituality that moves us to be involved" without specifying what shape this action must take.[24]

How should a faith community pray together about social and political issues? "Carefully," responds Mary Eaton, who experienced firsthand the tensions within the congregation. Communal prayer "should reflect that which can be lifted collectively."[25]

Experiences in Other Congregations

To be sure, many people do not see much connection between Sunday worship and social or political concerns. Some congregations focus worship almost exclusively on the individual's personal relationship with Jesus, with little connection to the larger world. One Southern Baptist woman said, for example, that in her experience "the primary emphasis in congregations is on salvation of souls, which sometimes leads to neglect of compassion and [also of] concern for broader social issues."[26] At the other extreme, in some congregations prayer may sound like a partisan political commercial. One United Methodist pastor in the New England Annual Conference, for example, expressed concern with church prayers that "wrap God in a flag."[27]

I live in Massachusetts, a state recently embroiled in contentious debate about whether same-sex marriage should be legalized. The Boston Roman Catholic archdiocese strongly opposed legalization of gay marriage. Church teachings unambiguously defined marriage as the union of one man and one woman. My parish at the time was a somewhat progressive suburban congregation. Church members held differing opinions about gay marriage. Our pastor publicly supported respect for gay persons and spoke of the faithfulness of gay and lesbian couples raising children within our community; he debated critics in the local newspaper. How would we pray together about this issue—as Catholics—in Sunday worship?

The Mass includes time for intercessory prayer, particularly in the Prayer of the Faithful that follows the homily. This is the space for prayers for the nation, for our leaders, for the poor, for the sick, and for a variety of other concerns. As state legislators debated new law, as talk shows and political debates jockeyed for position, as supporters and opponents rallied in front of the state house, week after week we prayed these words: "We pray for a just, true, peaceful, and compassionate resolution of the debate on the definition of marriage." It was a way of praying into which all members of the congregation could join, however differently they might understand the nature of a true marriage. The prayer affirmed that Christians are called to practice justice even as they engage in a spirit of peace and compassion. It did not define "the truth" but noted that a question of truth was at stake in the debates. The prayer was humble in the face of a new and complicated public policy question. Yet critics on both sides might say that it was too vague, that it should have spelled out church teaching more clearly, or that it should have explicitly prayed for the full rights of gay persons to marry. How do we prayerfully engage social and political issues without simplifying those issues, or causing greater alienation or division in the faith community?

It can be particularly challenging to lead prayer in a diverse community. One UCC minister in Massachusetts struggles with this question. He believes that it was his role as pastor to help people "break free of individualistic views on prayer." But how can he lead prayer about those larger, often controversial social and political questions? How does he pray with integrity about issues on which he has strong beliefs, while still praying on behalf of the community? This man describes the pastor's role as "murky." The challenge of leading prayer is "a bit of a dance and not always a creative tension, sometimes a debilitating tension in being so vague that the prayer doesn't mean anything."[28]

"WHOA, UNITY SEEKERS!"

A month after the petition landed on Pastor Schaper's desk, the congregation established a Unity Committee, comprising three signers of the petition and three members who felt otherwise. The aim was to grow in understanding of one another's viewpoints, spiritualities, and needs. The committee would be a microcosm of the whole congregation. If they could come to authentic understanding and friendship, acknowledging their differences, so too perhaps could the wider community.

Rev. Schaper keenly felt the pastoral challenge she faced. She believed deeply that social and political action was part of the church's mission; spirituality should not be disconnected from the demands of seeking justice on specific issues. She rejected an otherworldly spirituality. Nevertheless, this was a community divided. Some of her flock did not feel nurtured. What was the pastor's role? Schaper tried to talk with all concerned. She was aware that her congregation needed to be able to turn to her in their own moment of crisis. She would be called upon to counsel or conduct funerals for their families, to be there in a nurturing, nonthreatening way. But she believed that concern for unity in the church must not get in the way of a struggle for justice. As she reflected in a church newsletter: "Whoa, unity seekers! Unity is a punctual concern, always emerging at times of tension and getting in the way of impatience about justice. We are not to rock the boat. Why? Because of unity. What we need more than unity is strong institutional hinges that open wide the doors to justice. A strong spine also helps. There is plenty of room for unity behind justice's urgency."[29]

How does a fractured community live and pray together as the church? What is true Christian unity? Surely it cannot be a surface unity that depends on not rocking the boat or on praying in vague terms that have little meaning. It must be a more genuine encounter amid difference, a deeper oneness amid diversity in the Spirit, a communion that makes space for all kinds of genuine prayer in a spirit of humility.

After several years in Coral Gables, Pastor Schaper expressed a sense that the "church," with its concerns for unity, was not adequately risking itself for justice. In June 2004, she resigned from her position as pastor of CGCC. She cited family concerns as the reason for her resignation; it was time to rejoin her husband, with whom she had been managing a long-distance commuting relationship for several years. However, her letter of resignation strongly signaled her frustration and growing sense of a call to social activism:

> In a time of free market fundamentalism (I love the free market when it is open) and aggressive militarism (there is a place for militarism in the world as long as violence is not our only strategy), escalating authoritarianism (did we really receive

a free speech award for holding a conversation?),
I find that I am called to major in justice and
minor in church for the coming period. We live
in a period when an irregularly elected President
is presiding over two undeclared wars, giving
away the national treasury to the rich, hurting the
environment and calling those of us who oppose
him unpatriotic.

She described her emerging sense of vocation: "I sense
that God is calling me to a more active and truly patriotic
role in matters such as these. They are not 'political' so
much as spiritual actions on behalf of God's certain justice and peace."[30]

Schaper left Coral Gables and took a position as
director of the Women's Fund of Western Massachusetts,
an organization dedicated to increasing philanthropy that
benefits women and girls. The Women's Fund is not religiously affiliated. A little over a year later, she went back
to church ministry, assuming the post of senior minister at
Judson Memorial Church, a socially active peace church
in the heart of Greenwich Village, New York City.

COMMUNITY CONTINUES
TO STRUGGLE

Meanwhile, the congregation in Coral Gables continues to
struggle to build community and discern its mission.
Members lament the lack of space for respectful dialogue.
They describe a caution that has crept into the congrega-

tion, a fear of talking about controversial issues because of the divisiveness that may surface. At the same time as it searched for a senior minister, the community conducted a survey of members and tried to recognize their varying needs. The desired qualities listed for the senior minister included both "ability to help members develop their spiritual life" and being "committed to social justice and community issues." Tellingly, the Pulpit Search Committee described the ideal candidate as one who has "the ability to unite a congregation which is diverse in membership and expectations concerning the mission of the church."[31]

Chapter 4

PRAYING IN THE SPIRIT OF THE PROPHETS: SOUTH AFRICA UNDER APARTHEID

———

I magine it: congregations across South Africa would rise up in prayer one Sunday in June, rise up like prophets from their pews. After decades of oppression and violence under apartheid, the people would raise their voices to God, praying for an end to unjust rule. As they remembered the black students murdered in an uprising a decade earlier, as they remembered all who had lost their lives in resistance to the state, they would call on God to remove the government from power.

This was the vision of a group of South African church leaders in 1985. It was as if prayer would finally give voice to the deepest hopes of the oppressed. No longer mincing words, no longer waiting on some solution not yet arrived, the people would call on God to take down the government. It would be, these leaders thought, a prophetic stance. For too long, the South African people had suffered under apartheid, an official system of racial segregation and discrimination that oppressed blacks and "coloureds" (persons of mixed race) since its institution in 1948. Many of the churches issued statements condemning apartheid, and some declared apartheid to be a heresy. Christian leaders in the South African struggle for liberation were clear: apartheid was against God's will.[1] But change did not come. It was time for the people to pray the government out of power.

Or was it? The call for prayer turned out to be highly controversial. Theologians and church leaders debated it; newspapers printed a running stream of controversy. What was prophetic to some was, to others, going too far, wrong-headed, presumptuous. The prayer, said critics, presumed to know—and to tell God—the one solution to the intolerable situation of apartheid. It could interfere with the church's ability to negotiate change in the government. It went against scriptural exhortations to obey and pray for civil authorities. It could incite people to violence against the state. It was not surprising that defenders of apartheid resisted the call to prayer. More difficult was the painful, public split among church leaders working for the same anti-apartheid cause. What was at the heart of this controversy? How do we pray in an evil situation that does not appear to change, despite all our efforts?

The South African situation under apartheid cannot be equated with American political disputes in a democratic context. Even so, the issues at stake in this story may

LORD, HAVE MERCY

find resonance with conflict closer to home. Christian congregations regularly pray during Sunday worship for government leaders. An organization called Presidential Prayer Team has, through its popular Website, enlisted millions of people to pray daily for the president of the United States, his cabinet, and military leaders. Behind these practices are beliefs that a Christian way of life entails prayer for the government. Of course, some Christians would also sharply condemn the policies, behavior, and rhetoric of their government officials. How do we reconcile these two stances? How do we pray for a government with which we profoundly disagree? Is it possible to be prayerfully prophetic vis-à-vis the government?

REMEMBERING A TRAGIC DAY

Hector Pieterson was thirteen when he was gunned down by state police on the streets of Soweto, a black township near Johannesburg, in June 1976. He was one of thousands of young students protesting the apartheid laws, particularly a decree to make Afrikaans (the language of the white minority) the official language in schools. Youths had taken to the streets in what began as a peaceful protest. Police came and, by many accounts, began shooting without warning at the students. "I saw a child fall down. Under a shower of bullets I went for the picture. It had been a peaceful march, the children were told to disperse, they started singing 'Nkosi Sikele' [a South African hymn and anthem of the resistance movement]. The police were ordered to shoot," recalls the photographer who captured the horrifying image of a young man carrying the dying Hector in his arms, his anguished sister Antoinette at his side. Antoinette, who was seventeen at the time, remembers the day vividly: "There were younger children at the march who shouldn't have been there. I don't know why they were there—Hector was one of them. . . . Then I saw a group of boys struggling. This gentleman came from nowhere, lifted a body, and I saw the front part of the shoe which I recognized as Hector's."[2]

Violent confrontations continued throughout the day, as police dropped tear gas on the young people, some of whom were throwing stones and burning buildings. By the end of the day, hundreds of students were dead and many injured. Riots spread throughout South Africa. The event became deeply etched in South African memory, a lightning rod for the anti-apartheid movement. So it was that June 16 was chosen as the day for a new prayer in the churches.

"PRAY THEM OUT OF EXISTENCE"

In 1984, a fiery black pastor named Rev. Allan Boesak stood before the national conference of the South African Council of Churches and issued a rallying call. Boesak grew up in South Africa and knew how deeply segregation penetrated even his own church; he served as pastor of the coloured branch of the Dutch Reformed Church. Boesak came to head the World Alliance of Reformed

Churches and was a leading figure in the anti-apartheid movement. He had helped to persuade the World Alliance of Reformed churches to declare apartheid a heresy, and now he pressed the churches further: "I call on all Christians and churches to set aside a day on which to pray for the downfall of this government. If the rulers will not hear the cries of the people, if they will not change, if they continue to prevent justice, let us pray them out of existence."[3]

The horror of the Soweto Uprising lingered in South Africa. The apartheid government continued its oppressive policies, depriving the majority of South Africans of the rights to vote, live where they chose, and get adequate education, health care, and employment. After P. W. Botha became president in 1984, the government intensified campaigns of discrimination and violent repression. The state banned all anti-apartheid organizations, outlawing all opposition. State security forces intimidated, tortured, and murdered many anti-apartheid activists.

The church was one of the few organizations capable of mounting a resistance to the South African government during this time, and the leadership of the ecumenical South African Council of Churches took up the charge. From its establishment in 1968 through the next two decades, the SACC was a strong force in the struggle against apartheid. In the 1980s, it stood in the forefront of resistance, marshalling its energies against the apartheid government, calling for international economic sanctions, taking a dangerously overt political stance. The church organization understood itself as living out a prophetic role. It stood against a ruling power that it denounced as unjust and heretical.

Looking at the dire situation in 1985 and remembering the events of June 16, 1976, a group of SACC leaders coalesced around the idea of praying for an end to unjust rule. They published a theological rationale for the prayer and then issued a call to Christians across the country: pray for the removal of the government when you gather in worship on June 16, 1985. Enough was enough, went the argument: "We have prayed for our rulers, as is demanded of us in the scriptures. We have entered into consultation with them, as is required by our faith. . . . We now pray that God will replace the present structures of oppression with ones that are just, and remove from power those who persist in defying his laws, installing in their place leaders who will govern with justice and mercy."[4]

The argument for the prayer alludes to the Pastoral Epistle 1 Timothy, which expressly counsels the Christian community to pray for kings and all those in authority: "First of all, then, I urge that supplications, prayers, intercessions, and thanksgivings be made for everyone, for kings and all who are in high positions, so that we may lead a quiet and peaceable life in all godliness and dignity. This is right and acceptable in the sight of God our Savior" (1 Timothy 2:1–3). How do we reconcile this Scripture with a prayer for an end to the government in South Africa?

Scholars debate the authorship and dating of 1 Timothy; many believe it was not written by Paul himself but rather in the early part of the second century. What is certain is that the letter emerges from a particular social context and that it counsels Christians about how to survive and live peacefully under Roman rule. At a time when Christians faced the very real danger of persecution or execution, the author advises them, in effect, to lie low, avoid wrangling with the authorities, and instead pray for them. However, even though the letter presumes that the civil authorities deserve a certain honor and that the political order is not counter to God's will, prayer for the authorities also places them under the sovereignty of God. Indeed, the author praises a higher king than any earthly authority: "To the King of the ages, immortal, invisible, the only God, be honor and glory forever and ever" (1 Timothy 1:17). It is, then, a careful word of counsel for Christians living in a particular situation. What might this letter to an early Christian community say to South African Christians under apartheid?

REJECTING A STATUS QUO SPIRITUALITY

It did not require Christians to be passive collaborators with an evil government, argued South African theologians such as John de Gruchy. Nor did it call for a privatized, otherworldly spirituality separated from politics, a supposedly neutral kind of prayer. The question is not whether prayer and politics should be tangled together; they already are, asserted de Gruchy. He pointed out that such state functions as opening a legislative session and sending out troops often wove prayer and politics together. Political prayer was nothing new; religion often served the authorities in power. The Dutch Reformed Church in South Africa, for example, had supported the apartheid government, even giving the system of racial segregation a theological justification.

The call for prayer to end unjust rule was therefore not some new political kind of prayer. It was startling only because it prayed for change, because it was critical and prophetic. As de Gruchy wrote: "What is new for many people is that prayer should no longer be harnessed in support of those in power and the maintenance of the status quo, but in the service of the transformation of society. This does not mean that Christians should no longer pray for those in authority, but that they should pray for them on the basis of what the kingdom of God requires of rulers. The priestly, prayerful service which the church renders to the state cannot be separated, as Karl Barth shows, from its prophetic responsibility."[5]

Supporters of the prayer to end unjust rule called on Christians to integrate their piety with their political life, to abandon what they saw as an unbiblical, other-worldly spirituality. South African theologian Charles Villa-Vicencio wrote that the biblical tradition "knows no gap between the sacred and the secular, between prayer and social engagement."[6] When Christians falsely believe that they are keeping their spirituality untouched by politics—keeping it "private"—they end up supporting the status quo. De Gruchy lamented the "Christian sanctification of apartheid, and the unbiblical privatization of piety which has separated prayer and the struggle for justice."[7]

Surely, though, South Africans must have wondered whether their prayer would do any good. The government seemed so entrenched. The people had suffered under apartheid for decades, and nothing seemed to change the

LORD, HAVE MERCY

situation. South Africans continued to bury their children, their husbands, their neighbors. How could they continue to pray as a situation of suffering persisted? The people must have wondered: Where is God? Why is God silent?

South Africans did not come up with easy answers. Many did pray with hope and determination. After decades of oppression under apartheid, political change might have seemed nearly impossible to achieve. Still, wrote Villa-Vicencio, one should pray even for what seems impossible at the present moment. Christians live in hope. Said Villa-Vicencio: "If politics be the art of the possible, then prayer is the quest for what is not immediately possible but may be possible tomorrow. Such is the nature of Christian hope." For the theologian, prayer is an "eschatological symbol"— not encouraging passive wishing or waiting but rather calling one forward to work under God's grace for what one prays, so that, in the words of the Lord's Prayer, "thy kingdom come." Prayer is not "otherworldly" in any way that would entail disengagement from this world or acquiescence to the way things are. Rather, prayer actively seeks to bring about the world we hope for. Prayer leads us to reexamine our commitments. It becomes a "lure drawing one forward to the end for which one is praying."[8]

VOICES OF CAUTION

This lure to action was exactly what some feared in the call for prayer to end unjust rule. Critics argued that the prayer could unintentionally incite violence, encouraging people to take matters into their own hands and try to remove the government by force.[9] We need to be careful, they said, about the kind of action to which our prayer leads. Was this just another expression of the passive, status-quo-supporting church? Or was this a correct word of caution?

The Anglican Archbishop of Cape Town, Rev. Phillip Russell, was one of those who thought caution was appropriate. Russell opposed apartheid, but he did not support the prayer for an end to unjust rule. He worried about the implications of such a prayer. What would it mean to stop praying *for* the government, he asked, and to pray instead for its removal? Russell argued that one cannot negotiate with a government when one is asking God to remove it from office. If the church entered into this prayer, then it would need to stop its efforts to meet with and influence the government. This could be, he thought, an imprudent step. Russell also noted that the prayer would require a change in the South African prayer book and liturgy. He felt the call had a scriptural justification but, given the profound implications, he refused to commit the Church of the Province of South Africa to it. Instead, he called on the highest courts of the Anglican church to deliberate about the matter.[10]

Peter Storey, the head of the Methodist church in South Africa at the time, also opposed the call to prayer, even though he heartily agreed that Christian spirituality and struggle for social justice go hand in hand. Storey had long held a strong stance against apartheid and worked to bring about peaceful change. Though a white native South African, he was no stranger to the horrors of apartheid. He had ministered for many years in the inner cities of

LORD, HAVE MERCY

Cape Town and Johannesburg and served as chaplain to Nelson Mandela at Robben Island, the notorious prison for political opponents to the nationalist government. In the 1980s, he urged the international community to take stronger action against the apartheid government.

Nevertheless, Rev. Storey did not support the prayer to end unjust rule. It went against his theology. He believed that the prayer tried to limit God, that it dictated to God one and only one way to change the situation in South Africa. Storey later wrote: "In terms of the Methodist doctrine of grace, I did not believe that we were committed 'to pray prayers which limit the operation of that grace to one option only.' While God might well decide upon that option, 'it is not our business to limit him to it.' "[11] Some other theologians concurred, saying that the prayer to end unjust rule contradicted Scripture and tradition and was "presumptuous both in its approach to God and to the churches of God."[12]

PRAYING IN THE SPIRIT
OF THE PROPHETS

Was it presumptuous to pray for the end of the government? Or was it boldly prophetic? What would it mean to pray in the spirit of the prophets?

The biblical prophets repeatedly bring God's word of judgment to those who oppress, who abuse and scatter the people of Israel, who pay unjust wages, who maltreat orphans and widows. "Woe to him who builds his house by unrighteousness, and his upper rooms by injustice" proclaims Jeremiah (22:13). Writing during a horrible time in Israel's history—during and after the Babylonian sack of Jerusalem—the prophet brings God's word of justice and deliverance to those who are suffering and oppressed. Jeremiah also clearly signals that true prayer must correspond with a just life. The text depicts a God who has no patience for prayers from a faithless, evil people. In anger, the Lord says: "Do not pray for the welfare of this people. Although they fast, I do not hear their cry, and although they offer burnt offering and grain offering, I do not accept them" (Jeremiah 14:11–12). Prayer disconnected from a just life does not move God. The prophet relays the Lord's command: "Execute justice in the morning and deliver from the hand of the oppressor anyone who has been robbed" (21:12). The prophetic tradition strongly critiques false worship and idolatrous, hypocritical prayer.

Anti-apartheid leaders saw themselves as following in this prophetic tradition. Just a few months after the call for prayer was issued, a group of South African theologians published *The Kairos Document,* which sharply critiqued what it called "state theology"—a "blasphemous" attempt to give a racist, oppressive government theological justification. The document described proponents of state theology as "false prophets." It also denounced what it called "church theology," the inadequate responses of the English-speaking churches that sought reform and reconciliation with the state, compromising with rather than confronting structural injustice. Why have the churches not developed an adequate social analysis and political strategy to combat apartheid? queries the document.

> The answer must be sought in the type of faith and spirituality that has dominated Church life for centuries. . . . Social and political matters were seen as worldly affairs that have nothing to do with the spiritual concerns of the Church. Moreover, spirituality has also been understood to be purely private and individualistic. And finally the spirituality we inherit tends to rely upon God to intervene in his own good time to put right what is wrong in the world. That leaves very little for human beings to do except to pray for God's intervention. It is precisely this kind of spirituality that, when faced with the present crisis in South Africa, leaves so many Christians and Church leaders in a state of near paralysis.

In contrast, the *Kairos* authors advocated a more radical, "prophetic theology"; they argued that Christians need to make a "bold and incisive response that is prophetic, a response that does not give the impression of sitting on the fence but is clearly and unambiguously taking a stand." As opposed to the false spirituality that separates faith and politics, prophetic theology is infused with "a truly biblical spirituality [that] would penetrate into every aspect of human existence and would exclude nothing from God's redemptive will." Prayer is part of a prophetic response, but prayer cannot simply serve the "need of the individual for comfort and security." The prayer of the community, rather, "must be reshaped to be more fully consistent with a prophetic faith." Prayer must explicitly name the evil forces operating in South Africa, and it cannot be separated from active participation in the struggle for liberation, civil disobedience, and mobilization of all Christians to work for a change of government.[13]

As one considers the language of *The Kairos Document* and the call for prayer to end unjust rule, one might ask: How does it make sense to talk of praying prophetically? Prophecy is a word directed to human beings; prayer should most directly address God. Yet one can begin to envision what it would mean to pray in the spirit of the prophets. Prophetic prayer calls out to the God who demands justice, trusting that God liberates God's people. Prophetic prayer is quite this-worldly, in the sense that prophets call for transformation in the here-and-now. They pray boldly in the face of injustice. Prophetic prayer has a critical edge—reading a situation keenly, naming what is unjust, and calling on God to deliver the oppressed. Prayer in the spirit of the prophets, moreover, flows into and out of a just way of life. The prophet prays and acts for radical revisioning of this world and of our own hearts. Would a call to be prophetic, then, necessarily lead to prayer specifically for removal of an unjust government? How specifically do any of us—prophets included—know the will of God?

Of course, we should be able to pray into and out of the particularity of our lives. God invites us to pray our heart's fiercest desires. A wonderful model of this prayer is the biblical Hannah, who desperately wanted a child. After years and years without hope, she presented herself before the Lord in the temple; deeply distressed, she wept bitterly as she prayed, quite specifically, for a male child. Her passionate, silent prayer attracted the attention of Eli, the temple priest, who presumed that she was drunk and confronted her. Hannah protested: "I am a woman deeply troubled; I have drunk neither wine nor strong drink, but I have been pouring out my soul before the Lord" (1 Samuel 1:15). The Lord remembered Hannah; she bore a son, the prophet Samuel. Faithful to her promises to God, she gave the child to the Lord's service and sang out her joy in God her savior. Like Hannah, we should be able to come before God with all of our selves, offering up our deepest longings, our anger, our conviction, our best judgment about what should happen in our lives. We may even be presumptuous, incorrect, off-centered, but God will sort it—and us—out. We trust that God will be God. Interestingly, in Hannah's story, it is through prayer that prophecy is born.

We do, moreover, have some reason to trust that even our inarticulate or garbled prayers may find God's ear correctly. In writing to the Romans, the apostle Paul gives us assurance that the Spirit will intercede for us according to the will of God as we do not know how to pray as we ought: "Likewise the Spirit helps us in our weakness; for we do not know how to pray as we ought, but that very Spirit intercedes with sighs too deep for words. And God, who searches the heart, knows what is the mind of the Spirit, because the Spirit intercedes for the saints according to the will of God" (Romans 8:26).

Still, as we pray in public, as the community of the church, purporting to be prophetic, there is a place for discernment. The Scriptures warn repeatedly that prophecy must be tested. In the Book of Jeremiah, God rails against the false prophets who lead Israel astray, who "speak visions of their own minds, not from the mouth of the Lord" (Jeremiah 23:16). The false prophet "presumes to speak in my name a word that I have not commanded the prophet to speak. . . . The prophet has spoken it presumptuously," warns the book of Deuteronomy (18:20–22). In the New Testament, the early Christian communities too are warned: "Beloved, do not believe every spirit, but test the spirits to see whether they are from God; for many false prophets have gone out into the world" (1 John 4:1). False prophets will come to us like wolves disguised as sheep (Matthew 7:15).

The word *prophetic* can be used quite freely in religious circles to justify almost any political agenda. The Scriptures sound an important word of caution: beware of speaking as though you were relaying God's word, when you are merely speaking your own. You can easily deceive yourselves: "They say, 'Says the Lord,' when the Lord has not sent them, and yet they wait for the fulfillment of their own word!" (Ezekiel 13:6). The practice of discernment goes hand in hand with prophecy.

Discernment is a critical practice of faith. One needs discernment to pray well. At the same time, prayer over time hopefully deepens our capacity for discernment, expanding our ability to pay attention, listen, and align our will with that of God. The Lord's Prayer, for example, offers us words that, said again and again, can form us in humility and discernment: "your will be done." The Lord's Prayer invites us to ask for what we need, "our daily bread," yet also places those petitions ultimately under the larger hope that God's will be done, God's kingdom come.

MUST WE OBEY THE GOVERNMENT?

So, how do we pray boldly in the spirit of the prophets, yet with careful discernment, with conviction but also with humility about how we can know the will of God? In South Africa, the question came back again and again to debates about how to interpret scriptural texts that seem to counsel a docile attitude toward the government. Boesak describes how critics of the call for prayer to end unjust rule lifted up Romans 13, for example, as the basis of their opposition: "This call . . . caused a veritable controversy in the churches, upheaval in the secular world, and rising tides of fear and anger in the white Christian community. Once again I was the recipient of countless admonitions, in letters as well as (secular) newspaper editorials, to honour what is written in Romans 13."[14] Was the prophetic insistence on justice irreconcilable with this letter of Paul? As the Bible contains many voices, texts from diverse historical contexts, written for different purposes and communities, how does one draw upon them as one seeks to respond faithfully to a particular contemporary context?

The apostle Paul wrote the letter to the Romans around C.E. 55 or 56, during the early years of Emperor Nero's reign. The community in Rome experienced upheaval following Emperor Claudius's edict in 49, which expelled Jews from the city. Because many early Christians were Jews, like Paul himself, the edict and its subsequent repeal in 54 would have meant first exile and then return for a segment of the Christian community. Paul writes to the Romans in the wake of this upheaval. The letter appears to assume that

Praying in the Spirit of the Prophets

the civil order is part of the divine order, that the government gets its authority from God: "Let every person be subject to the governing authorities; for there is no authority
except from God, and those authorities that exist have been
instituted by God. Therefore whoever resists authority
resists what God has appointed, and those who resist will
incur judgment" (Romans 13:1–2).[15]

Did Paul's letter to the Romans counsel unquestioning obedience to government? Scholars debate this point,
with some arguing that Paul has been misinterpreted and
co-opted to support conservative positions.[16] Some would
assert that Paul delicately negotiated a space for the Christian community under Roman rule, pragmatically making
some compromises while relativizing civil authority and
pursuing the bold mission of proclaiming the gospel.
Clearly, this was Boesak's argument.[17] Still, the text was
a weight on the prophetic spirit. How could Scriptures
such as Romans 16 and 1 Timothy 2 be reconciled with a
prophetic spirituality that critiques and stands up to power?

In considering how to be faithful under apartheid, in
wrangling over the Bible, in discerning how to pray, some
South African church leaders and theologians looked to
the Reformed theologian Karl Barth. Barth was a pastor
and theologian teaching in Germany in the early 1930s. He
grew increasingly disturbed by the church's tolerance of
Adolf Hitler and so led a Confessing Church movement
that resisted the Nazis. In 1934, Barth helped to craft the
Barmen Declaration, which affirmed the autonomy of
the church vis-à-vis the state and rejected totalitarianism.
He was forced to leave Germany the following year when
he refused to swear allegiance to Hitler. Those experiences

deeply shaped his conviction that the church may well need to take a critical stance in relation to the state. In an essay entitled "Church and State," first published in 1939, Barth argued that Christians do have a duty to offer intercessory prayers for the state. He noted, however, that we do not pray *to* the state but rather to God on its behalf. The church should be like a priest in society. In its priestly function, the church must pray for the state, even and *especially* for a state that is not fulfilling its God-given function. Above all, the church must remain free. Thus, sometimes the church *must* criticize the state, even while praying for it. Barth writes: "Christians would be neglecting the distinctive service which they can and must render to the State, were they to adopt an attitude of unquestioning assent to the will and action of the State which is directly or indirectly aimed at the suppression of the freedom of the Word of God. . . . If the State has perverted its God-given authority, it cannot be honoured better than by this criticism which is due to it in all circumstances."[18]

In Barth's understanding, then, Christians could acknowledge the state's authority (Romans 13) and pray for the government (1 Timothy 2), all while exercising a prophetic critique born of Christian freedom.

PROPHECY OR PRESUMPTION: DISCERNING THE LINE

Much of the media coverage about the call for prayer focused on the debate among church leaders and theologians. Little is recorded about what ordinary people did on June 16, 1985. Did they lift up their voices in prayer, asking God to remove the government? Some would say that this idea was nothing terribly revolutionary in the black community, where people had long prayed for the dismantling of the apartheid state. For the highly public leaders of the faith community, however, it was indeed a difficult and painful moment, one at the heart of the relationship between sacred and secular, God's grace and human action, spirituality and politics. On the anniversary of the Soweto Uprising, in remembering many young South Africans such as Hector Pieterson, killed way before their time, what prayer would have been a faithful response to the urgency of the situation?

The South African story emerges from a situation of clear oppression. Many of the social and political questions faced in democratic societies are murkier, the "right" action even less certain. People of faith continue to wrestle with questions similar to those faced in South Africa. The South African supporters of the prayer to end unjust rule warn against an otherworldly spirituality that purportedly avoids politics but in avoidance ends up supporting whoever and whatever is in power. Others caution against presuming to know more than we can know and presuming to tell God how to act. Where do we draw the line between prophecy and presumption? With what specificity should we petition God?

Chapter 5

LAMENT AND RECONCILIATION: PRAYING THROUGH INJUSTICE

M atthew Goniwe was a thirty-eight-year-old teacher and anti-apartheid activist. Fort Calata led a youth organization; he was also the father of two toddlers and his wife was eight months pregnant with their third child. Sparrow Mkonto worked for the railroad. Sicelo Mhlawuli was a journalist and an old friend of Goniwe's. One night in June 1985, the four men traveled from the small town of Cradock in the Eastern Cape region of South Africa to a political meeting in the town of Port Elizabeth. They did not make it back. A week later, their burned and mutilated bodies were found alongside a road. They had been kidnapped, taken to a deserted area, and murdered. Their bodies were left alongside a road. Their car too was burned. The men became known as the Cradock Four. Although the government denied responsibility for their deaths at the time, it was later proved that seven police officers, reportedly acting on orders from the apartheid regime, had committed the crimes.

These brutal multiple murders would unleash rage at the apartheid regime and the state violence that enforced it—anger that erupted, for example, in the midst of prayer during a packed funeral service. How would healing come? How would the people of South Africa pray through such injustices? The Cradock widows grieved for their husbands, children for their fathers, communities for their leaders. One of the killers eventually sought forgiveness from the families and amnesty from the state. He prayed for the opportunity to meet the Cradock widows face to face. After the eventual repeal of apartheid and democratic election of a new government in the 1990s, the South African nation too would struggle to find a path to reconciliation, a path to a new future as a multiracial community. As the nation moved to find a new future, how would prayer make a difference within the excruciating human struggle for justice, peace, and reconciliation?

We recall that in the gospel of Luke, one of Jesus' disciples sees Jesus praying, goes up to him, and asks him to teach them how to pray. Jesus responds by teaching the disciples the words of what we today call the Lord's Prayer. The prayer includes a plea to God for forgiveness, integrally linked to our extending forgiveness to others: "Forgive us our sins, for we ourselves forgive everyone indebted to us" (Luke 11: 4). As we picture South Africa under apartheid, as we put ourselves in the shoes of the widows of the Cradock Four, this text stands out as particularly difficult. What might it mean to pray this familiar prayer amid great suffering and injustice?

In the gospel according to Matthew, in Jesus' famous Sermon on the Mount, Jesus teaches the crowds to learn something new, to move from loving one's neighbor and hating one's enemy to a new command: "Love your enemies and pray for those who persecute you" (Matthew 5:44). Many South Africans surely struggled with this teaching. How can contemporary followers of Jesus live into this text, despite unbearable political injustice? Jesus seems to integrally connect prayer and forgiveness. We cannot kneel to pray without also opening our hearts to those who have injured us. This is easily written but far more difficult to put into practice. How do people with legitimate, sometimes overwhelming grievances, pray their way through situations of injustice and conflict? It is a powerful question, whether we think of our personal friendships and family relationships or of seemingly intractable social and political conflict.

As I reflect on these questions, two images from the South African experience stand out in my mind. One comes from the funeral for the Cradock Four. It is the image of row after row of mourners standing with fists raised, singing a song that was both prayer and anthem of resistance: "Nkosi Sikelela iAfrika" (God bless Africa). The other image is set in a city hall building in East London, South Africa, during a hearing of the Truth and Reconciliation Commission (TRC) nearly a decade later, after the miraculous shift to a democratic South Africa. It is that of Nomonde Calata, widow of Fort Calata, collapsing on the stand with a "piercing wail" as she recounted her experience of the murder of her husband; and of Anglican Archbishop Desmond Tutu, chair of the TRC, in response drawing the gathering out of its stunned silence with a quiet hymn.

PRAYING WITH FISTS RAISED

In a soccer stadium on July 20, 1985, mourners buried Matthew Goniwe, Fort Calata, Sparrow Mkonto, and Sicelo Mhlawuli. Tens of thousands of South Africans, as well as many international journalists and diplomats, converged on the stadium in Cradock for the funeral. It was a liturgy of mourning charged with defiant political energy. One of the speeches hailed "Comrade Goniwe" as a "gallant martyr of our people." Nomonde Calata described a Communist flag and an African National Congress (the major opposition party) flag flying in Cradock that day. Matthew Goniwe's widow explained: "It was just in defiance, a statement which was being conveyed to the government that there's nothing you're going to be able to control anymore. I can't even explain that kind of spirit. It was a funeral, but it felt like it was a liberation day for many. I think that is what lifted me that day."[1]

It was precisely such liberation that the government feared. Under apartheid, funerals became not only healing rituals of prayer and consolation but also public spaces for expression of outrage and political demonstration.

With few other opportunities for political demonstration, a funeral served as a mixture of prayer, protest, and rallying call, in spite of fierce efforts at armed control and surveillance by state police. Yet these funerals were still gatherings of prayer. Former Methodist bishop Peter Storey recalls: "Funerals were the places where community anger could be most blistering and it was often the public prayers of church persons—some leaders, some local pastors—that held the line, affirming that anger, embracing the pain, holding it up to God and reminding everyone that God is not mocked."[2]

This was the case at the funeral for the men from Cradock. Prayer mingled with and held the community's anger, pain, and protest. During the funeral, Rev. Allen Boesak, who was then vice president of the South African Council of Churches, gave an impassioned speech calling for further resistance against apartheid. An American observer described the close of the funeral: "The pallbearers lifted the four coffins to their shoulders, and a procession of clergy led the way from the dusty stadium down to the village cemetery. On either side of the solemn procession, people stood eight and ten deep. Every one of them, *every single person,* had their fists raised. No one moved. The only sound in the crowd was the quiet singing of the black national anthem, *Nkosi Sikelela iAfrika.*"[3]

The song, composed by a black teacher in a missionary school in Johannesburg in the late 1800s, calls on God to bless the people of Africa and hear their prayers. Like the funeral itself, the song had become both prayer and symbol of resistance, both hymn and anthem of the opposition. Standing at the funeral, watching the coffins

Lament and Reconciliation

of the men from Cradock pass by, the people raised their fists and sang in the African Xhosa language words similar to these:

Lord, bless Africa
May her spirit rise high up
Hear thou our prayers
Lord bless us. . . .
Descend, O Spirit
Descend, O Holy Spirit
Lord bless us
Your family.[4]

The words rang out amid the rows of mourners standing with their clenched fists raised in the air.

LAMENT: CRYING OUT TO GOD

The image plays over and over in my mind. Certainly, this was an unusual situation—an eruption of prayer, rage, and political protest in one of the only spaces that could hold it. But there is something powerful here that speaks even outside those particular circumstances. Surrounded by unjust powers, wrong-headed government, or simply inexplicable suffering, what would it mean to pray "with fists raised"? Can prayer be full of rage? Is there something problematic in mingling worship with political protest? Can we even raise our fists in protest to God?

We may feel uncomfortable with prayer that is angry, raw, demanding, doubting, unsanitized. Yet this image of raised fists finds resonance in the ancient Hebrew prayer book, the Psalms. The Book of Psalms is a collection of prayers, often sung as hymns, written over a span of several hundred years. There are one hundred fifty psalms in the Bible; at least one-third are known as psalms of "lament." The lament psalms cry out to God from a place of suffering. Some raise up to God, often bitterly, the community's pain amid devastation—the destruction of the Temple, exile from Jerusalem, threats from enemies. They do not separate prayer from the lived situation, including the political plight, of the people. The political and the religious are deeply interconnected.

These psalms petition God for help against political enemies. They lament the cruelty of those in power. They cry out from exile. They question God's justice. They even accuse God of abandoning them. Psalm 44, for example, calls on God for help after the Israelites are defeated and humiliated by an enemy. God had saved them from their foes in times past, the psalmist grants, but this time God abandoned them: "Yet you have rejected us and abased us, and have not gone out with our armies. . . . You have made us like sheep for slaughter, and have scattered us among the nations" (Psalm 44:9–11). From a painful position of defeat, disgrace, and exile, the psalmist appears bewildered, angry, and even accusatory. Why would God let Israel be shamed? Why, after Israel had been faithful, would God turn away? This is the angry protest of a people who believe they have been wronged, certainly by their enemies, but also by the one whom they still proclaim to be their King and their God. Boldly, the psalm tells God, "Rouse yourself! Why do you sleep, O Lord? Awake, do not cast us off forever!" (Psalm 44:23). Like many psalms of lament, however, the prayer ends on a note of hope. The one addressed is still the God who can help and redeem the people. This is a God who can still show constancy, and the psalmist is bold enough to ask for it: "Rise up, come to our help. Redeem us for the sake of your steadfast love" (Psalm 44:26).

Here is a language for protesting injustice within a context of prayer. Here are words that give voice to questions, that give us a way to raise up suffering with anger and hope. "The community psalms of lament press us to consider how worship can, and indeed must, speak to a society and a globe that is beset by suffering," writes J. David Pleins, an American biblical scholar. The psalms of lament can "give the worshiping community a compelling vocabulary for confronting a God who oversees social dislocation and tragedy."[5]

Faced with persistent suffering and injustice, many would be tempted to stop praying. God does not answer. God does not intervene. Is there a God? What kind of a God do we have then? Those are important questions, not to be dismissed with an easy exhortation to "have faith." The psalms, however, perhaps like a South African funeral, give us a communal context of faith in which to ask the questions, a way to pray them alongside the voices of those who have prayed them before. In the language of the psalms, the questions can themselves be prayers. They are not matters we need to settle prior to prayer, so that we may pray. Prayer can debate with God, even accuse God. The psalms do not solve the problem of why suffering happens, but they do offer us a way to name the suffering and stay engaged with the world and God. Just as an argument can be a way to reconnect with the intensity of a relationship that has grown distant, so the psalms of lament may be a way to argue with God and thus reconnect with God despite difficult situations and troubling questions. We cry out. We challenge God. We demand relief. We affirm in the end that our hope is in God.

As the mourners in Cradock stood with fists raised, their song "Nkosi Sikelela iAfrika" may indeed have rung out like a psalm of lament, a strong protest against unjust suffering, a sharp call for God to descend and relieve the pain. Prayer merged protest against injustice, hope for liberation, and confidence that God ultimately would save.

Still, there is quite a bit of distance between the strong language of the lament psalms and Jesus' exhortation to forgive. How might Jesus' call be related, for example, to the shocking cry, in Psalm 137, for vengeance against the Babylonian captors who devastated Israel: "Happy shall they be who take your little ones and dash them against the rock!" (v. 9). Can the distance be breached? Can the psalms of lament be seen as one moment of prayer in a larger move toward reconciliation?

In the gospel of Mark, Jesus teaches his disciples about the power of prayer. Everything you ask and pray for, he says, if you believe in your heart that you have it already, will be yours (Mark 11:24). Directly following, he tells his disciples that prayer and the act of forgiving go hand in hand: "Whenever you stand praying, forgive, if you have anything against anyone; so that your Father in heaven may also forgive you your trespasses" (v. 25). The text does not offer us a glimpse into how the disciples responded to this difficult exhortation.

We may find it difficult to hear these Scriptures alongside the story from Cradock. In the defiant prayer of the raised fists, in the struggle for liberation, where does Jesus' teaching resound? These are shockingly difficult texts, jarring with the angry protest encapsulated in the image of the raised fist, jarring with the words of the violent, vengeful imagery of some of the psalm texts.

The dissonance is important to hold; it speaks truly to the complexity of living into the Christian faith, particularly in a situation of long-rooted political injustice. How do we balance the claims of justice and the rightful hunger for liberation with the gospel command to forgive? How do we forgive without dismissing terrible wrongs—wrongs often inflicted on people who can no longer speak for themselves? How do we pray into a future without abandoning the claims of the past?

Even today, these questions are unresolved for the people of South Africa. But we do find that within the South African community, over time, both prayerful protest and prayerful forgiveness have occurred. Desmond Tutu is widely regarded as an embodiment of both.

Tutu is an Anglican priest who was a vehement opponent of the apartheid system at its height. Beginning in 1978, when he became the first black general secretary of the South African Council of Churches, he used his leadership to strongly protest the apartheid system and generate international pressure—including economic boycotts—on the government. He was awarded the

Nobel Peace Prize in 1984. In 1986 he became the arch-bishop of Cape Town and thus the leader of the Anglican Church in South Africa. He continued to make it his mission to secure equal rights for blacks and coloureds, boldly defying state-imposed restrictions on political speech. As he presided over a funeral for anti-apartheid activist Irene Mkwayi in 1988, for example, he declared, "Apartheid is immoral, it is desecrating and it is filthy."[6] Even so, he also condemned any use of violence in the struggle against apartheid, insisting that the struggle would triumph because the cause was "just and noble."[7] Tutu was a bold symbol of spiritual strength in the struggle against apartheid. After the repeal of apartheid in the 1990s, he continued to draw from the wellsprings of faith as he led the country in a prayerful movement toward forgiveness and reconciliation.

MAY THE HOLY SPIRIT POUR OUT ITS GIFTS

After years of struggle, protest, prayer, and growing international political and economic pressure, democratic elections were finally held in South Africa in 1994. The people voted the apartheid government out of office and elected Nelson Mandela as president. The country then faced an enormous challenge: how to face the atrocities of the past while building a new, viable South Africa? They could not gloss over the violence and injustice. Nor could they afford to be continuously mired in civil strife from unending cycles of retribution. As a way forward, a compromise of sorts, Mandela established the Truth and Reconciliation Commission in 1995. The TRC had the power to grant amnesty to people who had committed crimes under the apartheid regime, if the perpetrators publicly and fully disclosed the facts of those crimes and if the actions evinced a clear political motivation.

The TRC erected a space in which the atrocities committed under apartheid could be named out loud and documented, so that the truth would be uncovered. The proceedings were open to the public and televised live. Victims and families told their stories. Those who committed crimes would also come before the commission, their victims, and the South African public to recount what they had done. The TRC tried to present itself as even-handed by investigating both state-sponsored violence and atrocities committed by resistance fighters; critics charged that this wrongly equated the actions of oppressors and oppressed. The hope nevertheless was that this sometimes controversial process would enable South Africa to move forward to democracy, healing, and reconciliation.

After many years as the public, spiritual leader of the anti-apartheid movement, Desmond Tutu, who was known and respected around the world, was the natural choice to chair the commission. Although he was nearing retirement and looking forward to some rest after decades of high-profile, high-pressure ministry, he accepted this new calling, which he understood as a deeply spiritual task. Tutu brought a religious presence and tone to the proceedings. Throughout the process, he wore his red archbishop's robe and cap, a clerical collar, and a large cross around his neck. He often led prayers and hymns to open and close the hearings. One author perceived this as a TRC "liturgy."[8] Indeed, despite the fact that South Africa was a religiously pluralistic country and the TRC was a government-established commission, Tutu did not hesitate to pray in explicitly Christian language. Some objected to the religiosity of the hearings. Tutu, however, came back again and again to prayer as a necessary part of the healing process. Once, in an early phase of the TRC, he attempted to begin a hearing in Johannesburg with only a moment of silence, rather than a prayer, at the request of colleagues. Before the first witness was called, however, he stopped and addressed the audience: "No! This is not the way to do it. We cannot start without having prayed." Tutu proceeded to pray that Jesus Christ, the "Truth," guide the process.[9]

As he opened the hearings in 1996, Tutu prayed for healing, repentance, justice, forgiveness, and reconciliation:

> We pray that all those people who have been injured in either body or spirit may receive healing through the work of this Commission and that it may be seen to be a body which seeks to redress the wounds inflicted in so harsh a manner on so many of our people. . . . We pray too for those who may be found to have committed these crimes against their fellow human beings, that they may come to repentance and confess their guilt to almighty God and that they too might become the recipients of your divine mercy and forgiveness. We ask that the Holy Spirit may pour out its gifts of justice, mercy, and compassion upon the commissioners and their colleagues

in every sphere, that the truth may be recognized and brought to light during the hearings, and that the end may bring about that reconciliation and love for our neighbor which our Lord himself commanded. We ask this in the holy name of Jesus Christ our saviour. Amen.[10]

Tutu did not have an easy job. Nevertheless, his confidence in a God of "justice, mercy, and peace"; in Jesus Christ calling us to reconciliation; and in the Holy Spirit bestowing gifts of justice and compassion gave him sustenance and hope. So prayer grounded him as he presided over the hearings, listening as South Africans told story after heartbreaking story of violence, grief, and anger.

A Widow Tells Her Story

One of the first victims to tell her story was Nomonde Calata, the widow of Fort Calata, one of the Cradock Four. She was only twenty and pregnant at the time of her husband's murder. She spoke of the day when she realized her husband had been murdered: "I looked at the headlines. And one of my children said: Mother, look here, the car belonging to my father is burnt.' At that moment I was trembling because I was afraid of what might have happened to my husband."[11] As she continued to speak before the TRC, Calata reached a point where, in Tutu's words, she "broke down with a piercing wail." The cry, he later wrote, "was the defining sound of the TRC."[12] As Calata sobbed, Tutu adjourned the proceedings for a few moments. When the hearing recommenced, Tutu began by singing the familiar chant "Senzenina" ("What Have We Done?"). Over and over, the hymn asks, "What have we done?" A South African theologian described the scene: "Everyone, even the journalists and security personnel, joined in the singing. Tears flowed."[13] This is the second image that sticks in my mind: Calata wailing in grief, Tutu leading the gathering in a responsive hymn.

Could prayer help Calata heal? Could prayer lead to reconciliation, opening South Africans to gifts of the Holy Spirit: justice and compassion? This was Tutu's vision; this was his prayer. As we follow the story of Nomonde Calata, we see the slow, tentative working of grace meeting up with still unresolved questions and long-standing heartache. Prayer was woven into the complicated search for accountability, humanity, and peace. It was, though, no instant solution to a legacy of political horror.

When Calata testified at the first victims hearing in 1996, no one stepped forward to take responsibility for the killing of her husband and little was known about how it occurred. Only later did seven former security policemen acknowledge responsibility and apply for amnesty through the TRC. One of those men, Eric Taylor, asked to meet with the families of the victims.

Calata had wondered for more than ten years: what happened to my husband that night in June 1985? Shortly after her husband's funeral, she gave birth to their third child, Thomani. Raising three children alone, she prayed every day that she would find some answers: "My prayer has always been to meet them (the perpetrators) so they could explain what they did and why. I prayed daily. Sometimes I got very angry, I feel they should take responsibility for caring for my children. I lost my job. I lost my husband, my friend, my children's father. I loved him." Now, she had an opportunity to sit face to face with the man who had killed her husband. She hoped to find answers. She agreed to meet with Taylor and told him: "But, thanks be to God that He has answered my prayers; that you have come to tell us these things, and to answer our questions."[14]

Taylor was a white South African who had joined the state police force when he was eighteen. In testimony he later gave to the TRC, he explained that he believed he was working to combat communism, and even to defend Christianity. He took for granted the correctness of the apartheid government: "I accepted that we are there to uphold the present government and Apartheid was part and parcel of the government at the time. There were a lot of values that I felt we had the responsibility to protect, and Christianity was, of course, one of those values. All the people that I worked with were Christians. You must remember that one of the elements of Communism is Atheism and that is the outstanding point, as far as I'm concerned, that actually justified the kind of work that we were doing."[15]

Taylor also detailed to the commission how he killed Fort Calata, hitting him behind the neck with a heavy metal object, and later pouring gasoline on him and burning his body. He said he understood the Cradock Four to be part of a "revolutionary onslaught" that he was charged to quell. The men were politicizing people,

LORD, HAVE MERCY

he said, stirring up dissent and violence. It was his job, under orders from some higher official, to assist in murdering them.

According to Taylor, he had a change of political perspective several years after the killings. It was a book that he read (the autobiography of Nelson Mandela) and a film that he watched (*Mississippi Burning,* about conditions in the American South) that began to turn his thinking. Taylor saw his actions in a different light. He expressed remorse for his part in the murders of the Cradock Four, and in the mid-1990s he decided to apply for amnesty and ask forgiveness directly from the families of the victims. He turned to his minister in the Dutch Reformed Church for assistance in arranging a meeting with the relatives of the Cradock Four. Incredibly, the families agreed to meet him. At that painful encounter, face to face with the relatives of the men he had helped to kill, Taylor told them what had happened to their loved ones. He explained his part in the murders, expressing regret and asking them "if they can find strength through God to forgive." He said that he was there "in response to God's prompting."[16]

Both Taylor and Calata prayed for this meeting, but for different reasons. One came to seek forgiveness; the other came to seek answers. Would prayer lead Taylor all the way to true repentance and transformation? Would prayer help Calata forgive? She told him: "Ah, Mr. Taylor, it is going to be very difficult for me to say that I forgive you, for what you did to me. Because you have caused so much pain to me and my family. You actually robbed my children from their father love. . . . He was everything to me."[17] The widow of Matthew Goniwe felt similarly: "I'm not going to absolve him, I mean, if he wants, you know, to feel lighter, I'm not the person who's going to do that. I refuse to do that. Umm, he can use, I mean, the TRC for that."[18]

The meeting did bring glimmers of hope. The son of Matthew Goniwe shook Taylor's hand in a gesture of forgiveness. Upon hearing of this "miracle of reconciliation," Tutu gave thanks to "the God of surprises."[19] Much of the work of reconciliation remained incomplete, though; the gap between Taylor and the Cradock widows still yawned.

Both women opposed Taylor's petition for amnesty. The families hired a lawyer to question Taylor and the other former security police during the TRC hearings. After extensive testimony, the commission refused Taylor's application for amnesty, concluding that the group had not told the full truth and not established a political motivation for all the killings.[20]

Taylor wondered how to explain all the publicity to his three children. He wondered how he would get past the past. The closest Calata and Taylor came to reconciliation was to recognize their shared humanity and a shared desire for peace. A film about their story, *Long Night's Journey into Day,* shows both at their respective churches—one a small black church, the other a white Dutch Reformed Church. Taylor says: "You can't live with this all your life. I just want to get it behind me and then, most important, is the fact that I would still like the families to one day forgive me." Calata says: "I mean, I'm a human being. I'm just a person like him. I will also want to overcome this thing. I don't want to live with it my whole life."[21]

Sharing in the "Divine Serenity, Sustained by a Cloud of Witnesses"

Tutu held the pain of many victims such as Nomonde Calata. He also heard from many such as Eric Taylor, who recounted horrible acts they had committed. In his book *No Future Without Forgiveness,* Tutu explains that he could not have done this work, could not have walked down this long and painful road in the hope of achieving some measure of reconciliation, without prayer. Prayer gave him calm, what he describes as a sharing in the "divine serenity." He would pray in the early morning, trying "to be quiet, to sit in the presence of the gentle and compassionate and unruffled One to try to share or be given some of that divine serenity. It was a mercy, too, to have the joyful privilege of a daily Eucharist."[22] Prayer gave Tutu stillness and strength in the face of turbulence. Prayer connected him to the One who abides beyond our present troubles. God was "unruffled"—not in the sense of untouched by suffering but rather wide and deep enough to hold and calm and see beyond the pain. Tutu believed God was deeply compassionate—literally, "suffering with." Prayer was a centering time of rest in the One whose hands were big enough to hold and settle all strife.

The prayers of others also sustained Tutu. He writes: "It was comforting, too, to know that we were being upheld by the fervent intercessions of so many in South Africa and around the world. Without all this I know I would have collapsed and the powers of evil, ever on the lookout to sabotage efforts to attain the good, would have undermined this extraordinary attempt to heal a wounded people."[23]

Intercessory prayer is prayer not for one's own needs but for others. In the gospel accounts, Jesus prays repeatedly for his followers, that they be protected from the evil one, that they be sanctified, that they live in God's truth, that all of them be one (John 17:9–23). He prays that through their unity others will believe in the gospel. He prays that his followers will always be with him: "Father, I desire that those also, whom you have given me, may be with me where I am, to see my glory" (John 17:24). Jesus' prayers for his followers express his love for them and his hope for their deepest well-being.

So too do the Pauline letters, the earliest writings of the New Testament canon, express belief in the power of intercessory prayer. Indeed, prayer for others flows from the nature of the church. As Paul explains to the divided Christian community in Corinth, the church is the "body of Christ." Paul urges the Corinthian community, which was beset by dispute, diverse loyalties, claims to spiritual authority, and sexual immorality, to "be united in the same mind and the same purpose" (1 Corinthians 1:10). The unity is not to be superficial but one that flows from baptism in the Spirit. All can retain their individuality and distinct gifts yet be joined, as hand to arm, in one body: "For just as the body is one and has many members, and all the members of the body, though many, are one body, so it is with Christ. For in the one Spirit we were all baptized into one body. . . . Now you are the body of Christ and individually members of it" (1 Corinthians 12:12–13, 27). The unity of the body engenders compassion. If any part of the body experiences pain, so too does the whole body experience pain: "If one member suffers, all suffer together with it" (1 Corinthians 12:26). It follows that the members of the body should pray for one another, as the author of the letter to the Ephesians counsels: "Always persevere in supplication for all the saints" (Ephesians 6:18). We pray because we experience the suffering of another in the body and lift that up to God as our own. In practice, intercessory prayer also builds compassion as we re-member those in the body.

In African terms, intercessory prayer affirms *ubuntu,* the interconnected nature of all reality, which Tutu pointed to over and over again. For Tutu, Christ's reconciling work resonated deeply with the African worldview captured by *ubuntu*: "My humanity is caught up, is inextricably bound up, in yours."[24] As chair of the Truth and Reconciliation Commission, Tutu relied on this sense of shared humanity and compassion. He also relied on the prayers of people around the world. Though reconciliation remained unfinished, Tutu was convinced that these prayers sustained the work of the commission: "Whatever we may have achieved is due in large measure to this cloud of witnesses surrounding us and upholding us."[25]

TEACH US HOW TO PRAY

These images remain: fists raised at the funeral of the Cradock Four, Nomonde Calata's piercing wail, Desmond Tutu and the TRC audience singing "What Have We

Done?" In the mix of these images, multiple expressions of prayer coexist: furious prayers of protest, overwhelmed cries of grief and horror and guilt, prayer that works its way into the divine serenity amid pain and conflict. What place does each have in the practice of faith, our slow and multilayered turning toward the gospel command to forgive one another and pray for our enemies? What prayer comes to the fore when you are distressed or wronged in your own situation? How have you experienced prayer along the difficult road to reconciliation? The disciple's request of Jesus was not answered once and for all, it seems. Instead, we continue to stand with the disciple, living into the same petition: "Lord, teach us how to pray."

Chapter 6

WALKING WITH OUR LADY: CESAR CHAVEZ AND THE FARM WORKERS

———

T hey carried Our Lady of Guadalupe right at the front of the procession. There, leading the line of farm workers and supporters, was a banner emblazoned with the icon of Our Lady, her hands clasped in prayer. Under her feet were printed the union initials NFWA (National Farm Worker Association). Alongside her walked a crowd of people on a march for justice, a long march over hundreds of miles from the dusty farm town of Delano to the state capitol in Sacramento. Red union flags waved in the wind alongside a wooden cross.

It was the spring of 1966, only one year since Martin Luther King Jr. led a nonviolent march from Selma to Montgomery, Alabama. This was a time of growing social consciousness and social unrest in the United States. The civil rights movement had gained strength and won some legislative victories, most notably the Civil Rights Act of 1964, which outlawed racial discrimination in public places and mandated equal employment opportunities. Still, race relations were extremely tense. Riots broke out in Watts in the summer of 1965. Growing student activism and the feminist movement added more voices to the public debate about equity and justice. The United States was beginning to send large numbers of troops to Vietnam.

It was in these charged times that a group of farm workers and their supporters set out from Delano in the hope of drawing publicity and support to their cause. They were among the poorest of the poor: Mexican and Filipino immigrants, many with no legal status or protection. They worked long hours under the hot sun for minimal pay, often under dangerous working conditions. They moved with the crops and enjoyed no stability or security. The story of how the workers came together into a movement is, in large part, tied to the story of Cesar Chavez, their leader.

Chavez grew up in a family of Mexican immigrants, working the fields. Born in Arizona in 1927, he met injustice early; when he was ten years old, he and his family were forced off the small farm that his grandfather had once homesteaded. They headed to California, where Chavez worked in the fields full-time after completing the eighth grade. He was strongly influenced by the traditional Catholicism of his Mexican family. He went to Mass. He learned to pray at his grandmother's feet. He revered Our Lady of Guadalupe. As a young adult, he also read the social teachings of the church and biographies of St. Francis of Assisi and Mohandas Gandhi. They shaped his faith, attracting him to service and nonviolence. As Chavez's story unfolds, these two parts of his life—the fields and his faith—eventually coalesce into one of the most important labor movements of the twentieth century.

Chavez's life took a turn in 1952 when he was working in an apricot orchard near San Jose, California. There he met a community organizer named Fred Ross, who persuaded Chavez to join him in trying to organize the Latino community. Chavez soon met Dolores Huerta, who later would become his partner in founding the United Farm Workers. Chavez, Huerta, and Ross worked across California during the 1950s, conducting voter registration drives and seeking to get poor Latinos active in the political process, meanwhile learning lessons about the power of grassroots organizing that would stay with Chavez throughout his life. In the early 1960s, he moved to Delano with his wife, Helen, and their eight children and began organizing farm workers full-time.

Organizing farm workers was far from easy. It entailed battling with large corporations that did not want to offer contracts and higher wages to the farm workers, as well as with the corporations' government allies. Ronald Reagan, for example, governor of California from 1966 to 1975, made a point of publicly eating grapes during the grape boycott. The farm workers also met stiff resistance from big, established unions such as the Teamsters. In 1965, the workers took a major step. A group of

Filipino American farm workers in Delano decided to strike, and they asked Chavez's fledgling union to join them. Chavez was ready to strike, but the workers themselves had to vote. Would they walk out? Would they picket their employers? To strike would mean no work, no wages. They had families to support, and the farm worker union had few financial resources to help them. On the day of the strike vote, more than a thousand workers jammed into Our Lady of Guadalupe church in Delano. It was September 16, Mexican Independence Day. The workers unanimously cast their votes in favor of joining the strike. The action would last five years and develop into an international grape boycott. It was symbolic that the strike vote took place in a church dedicated to Our Lady of Guadalupe, a powerful figure of hope, liberation, and God's special protection for many Mexican Catholics. She would become a center of devotion and a visible symbol of the farm worker movement.

According to tradition, in 1531 the Virgin Mary appeared to a poor Aztec Indian named Juan Diego on the hill of Tepeyac, near what today is Mexico City. It was a decade after the Spanish conquest had destroyed much of the Aztec civilization; the natives lived under colonial rule. Juan Diego was a baptized Christian, a widower, of simple background. He called himself "a nobody." As he was walking, he heard a voice calling him, beckoning him to climb the hill. He did and saw an incredible sight: Our Lady, her garments glimmering gold like the sun. Speaking to him in his native Nahuatl language, she called herself a "merciful mother" to him and all the people of Mexico and told him that she wished to show them her love, compassion, and solidarity in their affliction. She sent Juan Diego to the bishop to tell him that she wanted the bishop to build a church on the hill of Tepeyac.

Juan Diego summoned his courage to go to the bishop, who, however, rebuffed him in disbelief. Our Lady then told Juan Diego to climb the hill again, and he would find an assortment of beautiful roses to bring to the bishop as a sign. Though doubtful that he would find roses blooming out of the dry, craggy earth in the middle of winter, he followed her instructions. To his surprise, he found roses in abundance and filled his cloak with them. He returned to the bishop, who was astounded to see the roses fall out of his cloak and an image of the Virgin Mary appear on his clothing. Awed, the bishop built a church in Tepeyac in honor of Our Lady.[1]

For the Mexican people, the appearance was a religious event of extraordinary significance, giving them hope and dignity at a time of suffering and humiliation. Our Lady continues to symbolize liberation, the dignity of Mexicans, and divine solidarity with the poor. Today an enormous basilica of Our Lady of Guadalupe in Tepeyac draws thousands of pilgrims, who gaze at the cloak that still displays (behind bullet-proof glass) the image of Our Lady. Juan Diego was canonized in 2002.

Our Lady is the patron saint of Mexico. It is not surprising, then, that for Chavez and the farm worker movement, Our Lady of Guadalupe became a central symbol of divine blessing and solidarity. As Huerta expressed it, Our Lady was "a symbol of the impossible, of doing the impossible to win a victory, in humility. . . . I mean that's the important thing she symbolizes to the union: that with faith you can win. You know with faith you can overcome."[2]

MARCHING TO SACRAMENTO: BLISTERS AND BLOODY FEET

So it was that Our Lady of Guadalupe led the march to Sacramento, alongside Cesar Chavez, that spring of 1966. The workers had been on strike for months. Striking was hard and dangerous; the workers walked picket lines around farms, withstanding intimidation and violence: "Usually the ranch foreman and his staff would harass the strikers, reviling them with foul language, trying to provoke them into crossing onto farm property. Later the growers hired goons, recruited from the cities, to intimidate the strikers. Violence was a constant possibility and frequent occurrence. Ranch foremen raced their pickup trucks up and down the lines at top speed. They drove tractors between the pickets and the fields to choke the union people with dust. They sprayed them with chemicals and tried to intimidate them with shotguns and dogs. Sometimes they injured strikers."[3]

The striking farm workers were tempted to respond with violence, and some did. They also put their own pressure on strikebreakers, workers who would cross the picket line to take their jobs. Chavez grew increasingly convinced that the movement had to hold to nonviolence or it would lose its soul. In the turbulent decade of the 1960s, when many in the civil rights and student protest

LORD, HAVE MERCY

movements were drawn to nonviolence while others doubted its efficacy, Chavez saw nonviolence as important to the movement's success.

The march was a dramatic effort to publicize the farm worker cause and gain support for the grape strike. It was a demonstration for contracts and better wages and working conditions. It was a kind of civil rights march. It was also, in the word used by Cesar Chavez, a *peregrinación,* a pilgrimage, an act of penance to recommit the movement to nonviolence.

Chavez saw the march as a penitential practice for the workers, fitting during the season of Lent. Lent is a forty-day season of repentance, prayer, and spiritual preparation, modeled on Jesus' forty days of prayer, fasting, and temptation in the wilderness (Matthew 4:1–11). It is a time of renewal and cleansing, opening with hope into the celebration of Easter. In this spirit, Chavez set out in March 1966 to walk hundreds of miles to Sacramento. The pilgrimage was to cleanse the movement of temptations to violence; it would be "public penance for the sins of the strikers, their own personal sins as well as their yielding perhaps to the feelings of hatred and revenge in the strike itself."[4] For Chavez, the spiritual dimension of the struggle was critical. He did not want to simply lead a union; in his mind, the union was to be a spiritual community. The movement needed recentering. The march from Delano to the state capitol would publicly reassert the spiritual nature and nonviolent character of the struggle; it would serve to strengthen the workers. This was Chavez's hope.

The farm workers' pilgrimage was painful. Angie Hernandez Herrera, who walked the entire length of the

Walking with Our Lady

march, recalled: "Some people had bloody feet. Some would keep on walking, and you'd see blood coming out of their shoes."[5] Chavez himself suffered from severe foot blisters and had to receive medical care: "After the first couple of days his old shoes gave him blisters and one of his feet swelled considerably. Since he considered it a penitential walk, he refused to take medication to lessen the pain. By the end of the third day his leg was swollen and his blisters began to bleed. He was running a temperature. By the seventh day his physical condition was such that a nurse ordered him to ride in a station wagon, bitterly disappointed with himself. The next day he rejoined the marchers."[6]

Christians have long associated pilgrimage with penance. Through the physical stress of the journey, one offers oneself to God and seeks to be cleansed from sin. One seeks a fresh start. This was Chavez's understanding. The march from Delano was a kind of physical purgation. It was, to use a term common in the history of Christian spirituality, an ascetic practice. The word *ascesis* literally means "training." Chavez said, "We wanted to be fit not only physically but also spiritually, and we wanted to stress nonviolence even more, build confidence, and have more visible nonviolent tactics."[7] Indeed, this was a public ascesis, marked by blood and sweat.

The suffering of the pilgrimage had a purpose. The farm workers believed that through suffering and penance they would cleanse themselves and find justice. The inner renewal and the outward demand for justice went hand in hand; each depended on the other. Every night, as the workers rested and prayed and rallied in towns along the way, organizer Luis Valdez read out "El Plan de

LORD, HAVE MERCY

Delano," a composition he had written for the pilgrimage. The plan included these words: "The pilgrimage we make symbolizes the long historical road we have traveled in this valley alone, and the long road we have yet to travel, with much penance, in order to bring about the revolution we need. . . . We seek our basic, God-given rights as human beings. Because we have suffered—and are not afraid to suffer—in order to survive, we are ready to give up everything, even our lives, in our fight for social justice. We shall do it without violence because that is our destiny."[8]

CHRISTIANS EVER RESTLESS

To go on pilgrimage is a practice common to many religious traditions. Muslims journey to Mecca; undertaking the *hajj* is one of the five pillars of Islam. The ancient Israelites journeyed to Jerusalem, drawn to the Temple as God's own dwelling place, the holiest of holy sites. For that place the pilgrim longed, anticipating it with joy, as we read in Psalm 84: "How I love your palace, Yahweh Sabaoth! How my soul yearns and pines for Yahweh's courts! My heart and my flesh sing for joy to the living God . . . happy the pilgrims inspired by you with courage to make the Ascents!" (Psalm 84:1–5, Jerusalem Bible translation). Jesus was one of those pilgrims as he journeyed to Jerusalem each year with his parents to celebrate Passover (Luke 2:41–42). He returned to Jerusalem riding on a colt, to celebrate his final Passover before the crucifixion (Mark 11:1–11).

The early Christians continued the practice of pilgrimage. They traveled to the tombs of martyrs. Journeys to the Holy Land became popular in the fourth century, when Emperor Constantine I designated sites in Jerusalem as the "way of the cross" (*via cruces*). Pilgrims walked along what they believed to be Jesus' footsteps, venerating the sites associated with his Passion. Many Christians made trips to sites associated with saints and miracles throughout the medieval era. Geoffrey Chaucer famously described one set of pilgrims in his book *The Canterbury Tales*. In fact, pilgrimages became so popular (and were so abused by papal authority who offered pilgrims indulgences) that the Protestant Reformers criticized the practice.

Pilgrimages remain popular today. People travel to Jerusalem and Rome, to Lourdes and Fatima, to Iona and Knock. What draws people to undertake a pilgrimage? Some seek healing, or a miracle, or time for reflection and renewal. Others want to experience the fervor and peace of Christians in other points in time. People often hope to encounter God in a holy place, to stand in a setting where God entered human history—for example, in Bethlehem and Jerusalem, in the places significant in Jesus' life. By going back to the beginning point of their faith, in a sense they hope to find a new beginning point for their own lives. The journey is an expression and deepening of faith, a time to pause, reflect, pray, and unite one's life with those who have come before.

Countless authors in the Christian tradition have referred to Christians themselves as "pilgrims," even when they don't literally travel. The word expresses the never-settled quality of the Christian life. Christians are always walking toward, hoping for, a transcendent reality that is present, but never wholly, in this world. They are restless; as Augustine wrote in Book 1 of his autobiographical work the *Confessions,* "You have made us for yourself, and our hearts are restless until they rest in You." Pilgrimage, then, is a tangible practice that expresses what is really the whole of Christian life.

INTERLUDE: AN IRISH PILGRIMAGE

I wanted to experience this sense of pilgrimage, so I went to an old place of pilgrimage in Ireland. It is a small island in the middle of a lake in Donegal, a place called Lough Derg. People from all over Ireland and some from abroad come to the island for a three-day pilgrimage, an ascetic experience of fasting, prayer, and penance. When they arrive on the island, the pilgrims take off their shoes. They walk barefoot for their entire time on the island, even as they walk in circles over rocks while reciting the required sets of prayers. The "exercises," as they are aptly called, involve a structured routine of prayers or "stations," which pilgrims complete walking in circles around penitential beds and the ancient cross of Saint Patrick. Called "Saint Patrick's Purgatory," the island is a place for penance, self-cleansing, self-emptying, and renewal. Pilgrims do not sleep at all the first night on the island, remaining in a prayer vigil throughout the night. They fast in preparation for arriving on the island and, once there, are permitted only one meal per day of black tea and toast. On the second day of the pilgrimage, they go to confession. Clearly, penance, fasting, and pilgrimage are closely linked in the Lough Derg experience. This they share with Chavez's spirituality.

Yet the two practices of pilgrimage were also incredibly different. Lough Derg could not be more austere and remote. It is a place to be apart—completely surrounded by water, hearing not a whisper of traffic, not a newspaper in sight. It is worlds away from Sacramento—the hub of state government, a city. The farm workers made pilgrimage to an economic and political center; at Lough Derg, pilgrims go to the margins. The Irish pilgrims stand at the cross of Saint Brigid, throw out their arms in the shape of a cross, and say three times, "I renounce the world, the devil, and the flesh." They may mean the world in the sense of what is opposed to the spirit, but the words still jar against Chavez's sense of spirituality. Would Chavez have renounced the world as he stood on the steps of the state capitol?

As we consider the Irish experience of pilgrimage, the question surfaces: Should we call the farm workers' march to Sacramento a pilgrimage? Whereas the destination of a pilgrimage typically is a holy site, here the destination is the center of state government. Chavez sought a kind of spiritual rededication and purification; the marchers clearly sought economic and political benefits as well—contracts with growers, improved wages, public support, political power. They were indeed somewhat successful in these aims. What began as a small group in Delano swelled to thousands as supporters joined the march to the state capitol. Supporters included many who did not share Chavez's religiosity but who did share his passion for the cause. They were Jews and Protestants and atheists, all walking there alongside the banner of Our Lady. Some objected to the prominent religious symbols or saw the piety as dispensable. Jerry Kirchner, for example, said that once the farm workers won contracts with the growers, "we won't need Our Lady."[9]

A few days before the procession reached Sacramento, the National Farm Workers Association secured a contract with a major company, the Schenley Corporation. Chavez briefly left the march to negotiate the contract. Then Governor Pat Brown had left town before they arrived at the state capitol, but the workers and supporters poured exuberantly onto the capitol steps on Easter Sunday. There they held a kind of rally. Dolores Huerta publicly demanded that the governor call a special session of the legislature to establish a collective bargaining law in California. Was this the climax of a spiritual journey?

TWENTY-FIVE DAYS
WITHOUT FOOD

The answer depends greatly on what one considers to be spiritual. How are "spiritual" and "secular" related? How can spiritual practice engage this-worldly concerns without becoming a political tool or mere performance?

The farm worker story continues to lead us into such questions. The boycott dragged on, and some within the movement advocated taking violent means to accomplish their goals. By 1968, Chavez again saw a need to turn to traditional prayer practices to renew the movement. He declared a fast to rededicate the movement to nonviolence: "There was demoralization in the ranks, people becoming desperate, more and more talk about violence. . . . I thought I had to bring the Movement to a halt, do something that would force them and me to deal with the whole question of violence and ourselves. . . . So I stopped eating."[10] Chavez took inspiration from Gandhi, who fasted as a means of atonement and protest during the long struggle for Indian independence.

Chavez fasted for twenty-five days. He grew weak, barely able to walk. Supporters rallied around him. The fast strengthened support for the grape boycott and quelled internal debate about using violence. It also was a risk. Many were concerned that Chavez would die and leave the movement in disarray. Certainly, his wife Helen feared for their eight children. Secular liberal union supporters such as Saul Alinsky found the fast puzzling or even "embarrassing."[11] Some saw Chavez as playing martyr. The fast surfaced existing tensions within the movement as to its religious dimensions: "Some of the union's other leaders refused to talk to Cesar because they thought the fast was an absurd waste of time. Tony Orendain, who thought the fast was religious folly, sat with his back toward Chavez when they discussed union business. Other volunteers found the mystical and Catholic character of the fast so offensive that they also quit, complaining that Chavez was developing a messiah complex."[12]

Here arose two questions: Would the fast be "success-ful" (as opposed to a waste of time)? What place did a religious fast have in a diverse social movement anyway?

Huerta described the meaning of the fast in this way: "I know it's hard for people who are not Mexican to understand, but this is part of the Mexican culture—the penance, the whole idea of suffering for something, of self-inflicted punishment. . . . Cesar has often mentioned in speeches that we will not win through violence, we will win through fasting and prayer." Chavez saw no dichotomy between his spiritual practices and his prophetic work: "I said to myself, if I'm going to save my soul, it's going to be through the struggle for social justice."[13]

As described in many scriptural texts, fasting is a practice of turning around, repentance, an opening into the divine mercy. In the story of Jonah, for example, we read of how God sent this reluctant prophet to the enormous city of Nineveh to speak out against its evil ways. After Jonah defied God's command and fled in the opposite direction to Tarshish, and after God rescued him in the belly of a fish, Jonah finally went to the city and declared that it would be overthrown in forty days. The people of Nineveh listened and quickly sought to forestall God's wrath. They "believed God; they proclaimed a fast, and everyone, great and small, put on sackcloth" (Jonah 3:5). The king himself fasted. Even the animals, the king decreed, would fast. All would pray and turn from violence: "They shall cry mightily to God. All shall turn from their evil ways and from the violence that is in their hands" (Jonah 3:8). Much to Jonah's dismay, God did indeed relent and spared the people of Nineveh.

Although Chavez did not express fear of divine wrath as did the king of Nineveh, he did see human fasting, prayer, and repentance as turning away from violence and toward God. Of course, in the biblical story, God's mercy on Nineveh angers Jonah, because it does not square with Jonah's notion of justice. Chavez, on the other hand, saw his vision of social and economic justice as within God's own justice—and for this he prayed.

FRUIT OF THE VINE AND WORK OF HUMAN HANDS

Ever since I can remember, on Ash Wednesday, the first day of Lent, the church distributed alms boxes for us to take home. They were small cardboard boxes with a picture or two and a list of what our pocket change could buy in some other part of the world. The idea was that we would put money into the box throughout Lent. As we fasted from meat or other indulgences, the money saved would go into the box. Our fasting was linked to others' need, an expression of solidarity and outreach rather than simply a private devotion. As a girl, I don't think I quite understood all this, but I did get the idea that giving was supposed to go along with those fish Fridays. I proudly carried my little box filled with nickels and dimes back to church on Holy Thursday, to offer it alongside others as we commemorated Jesus' Last Supper and celebrated the Eucharist.

There is something fitting about breaking a fast with the Eucharist. Both in the fasting and in the partaking of the Eucharist, one affirms solidarity with others in the body and comes to a new appreciation of the gift of creation. It was natural, perhaps, then, that after twenty-five days, an extremely weak Cesar Chavez broke his fast by receiving the Eucharist at an outdoor Mass, surrounded by thousands of farm workers and supporters. The celebration of the Mass was an important prayer practice for Chavez and became central in the movement as well. Supporters gathered for Mass when Chavez was imprisoned. Union-friendly priests, wearing stoles with the UFW logo, said Mass with wine made from union grapes. What was the connection between the Eucharist and the *causa*?

The word *Eucharist* literally means "thanksgiving." At the Passover meal before his death (what Christians today call the Last Supper), Jesus took the cup and, only after giving thanks, offered it to his disciples and all drank from it (Mark 14:23). So too the celebration of the Eucharist includes both thanksgiving and sharing of bread and wine. The words of the Eucharistic Prayer in the Roman Catholic Mass express gratitude for the gifts of creation: "Blessed are you, Lord, God of all creation. Through your goodness we have this wine to offer, fruit of the vine and work of human hands." So too the prayer affirms the dignity of human work that cooperates with God's creative power; one can imagine that the words would have been particularly powerful for farm workers who spent countless hours in the heat picking grapes off the vine. Their work was blessed by God. The fruit of their labor would, in Catholic understanding, actually become the blood of Christ: "It will become our spiritual drink." As God is the giver of creation and continues to become present to the body in the everyday stuff of life, the thanksgiving of the Eucharist should lead to commitment to justice for all members of the community.

For Cesar Chavez, fasting was a way to repent and restore community when it was fractured and leaning toward violence. The celebration of the Eucharist affirmed that community and God's grace among us. Fasting and celebration of the Eucharist both witnessed to and anticipated God's justice. Chavez believed that the church is "one form of the Presence of God on Earth,"[14] called to be the servant of the poor. He knew that in reality the church does not live up to this sacred mission. In the early days of the farm worker movement, for example, Chavez found his own Catholic Church to be nonsupportive. This pained him, particularly in comparison with the strong backing the farm workers received from the Protestant California Migrant Ministry. Chavez developed an ecumenical understanding of the church. He was also clear that it is our responsibility to call the church back to the servant mission when it instead supports the rich and powerful. The church is to be with the powerless, the broken. Chavez invites us to celebrate the Eucharist as community, as Body of Christ, as church, called to stand with the poor and oppressed.

In practice, fasting and celebration of the Eucharist are often severed from this context of community and the call for justice. People fast with other motivations: as a legalistic observance of a church rule, as a way to wean oneself off bad habits, as a way to lose weight. We make fasting a badge of honor, announcing to all that we have given up cigarettes or chocolate or coffee. At the same time, we receive Communion and then quickly become impatient with the people pulling out of the church parking lot ahead of us. We pass by the homeless person outside the church with only an awkward glance away.

Chavez's fast and his devotion to the Eucharist resonated more with the call of the prophet Isaiah, which closely linked fasting with community and the practice of economic justice: "Look, you serve your own interest on your fast day, and oppress all your workers." The fast that is acceptable to the Lord is the one that cares for the suffering, care embodied, for example, in the sharing of bread: "Is not this the fast that I choose: to loose the bonds of injustice, to undo the thongs of the yoke, to let the oppressed go free, and to break every yoke? Is it not to share your bread with the hungry?" (Isaiah 58:3–7)

CHAVEZ'S FAST RALLIES SUPPORT

The fast that turns from violence and that does justice: this was the fast that Chavez undertook. His actions rallied enormous political support. Farm workers came from all directions to support him, pray for him, and commit themselves to the cause. Weak, on his bed, Chavez became a focal point for union organizing and religious fervor. As the authors of the book *The Fight in the Field* relate: "Some built shrines to the Virgin of Guadalupe at the union headquarters. Priests wore vestments cut from union flags and offered mass with union wine. People slept in tents they pitched in the yard and at night had festive prayer rallies with singing and hot chocolate. 'The irony of the fast was that it turned out to be the greatest organizing tool in the history of the labor movement—at least in this country,' says Leroy Chatfield."[15]

Here, in its secular success, lies a dilemma. When does fasting and prayer become a political tool, even a publicity stunt, the kind of self-serving display that Isaiah and the gospels both warn against? In the gospel of Matthew, Jesus commands his disciples to fast in secret, not looking gloomy, not seeking to gain the admiration of others. "But when you fast, put oil on your head and wash your face so that no one will know you are fasting except your Father who sees all that is done in secret; and your Father who sees all that is done in secret will reward you" (Matthew 6:17–18). Jesus was wary of public religious display, too often a hypocritical, empty outward expression. Chavez's fast was undeniably a very public, political act.

The popular Quaker spiritual writer Richard Foster draws a distinction between a fast and a hunger strike. He writes that one should fast for "spiritual purposes," whereas the purpose of a hunger strike is "to gain political power or attract attention to a good cause."[16] Here again, we come back to the underlying question that is so important to Christian practice: What is spiritual? Chavez would not have drawn the dichotomy that Foster does between spiritual and political. The political is necessary for achieving some measure of social justice, which God desires. Certainly, his prayer practice, whatever others in the movement made of it, seemed to spring from genuine piety. When, then, does a public display of spiritual practice—particularly in service of a political or economic cause—become inauthentic or misused?

WRESTLING WITH THE WITNESS

For Cesar Chavez, prayer was a way to turn back to God, again and again. Prayer recentered hearts in faith and non-violence. It cleansed and restored hope. In the farm worker movement, prayerful practices such as pilgrimage, fasting, and celebration of the Eucharist became powerful witnesses for social justice. For Chavez, prophecy without spirituality would be impossible. He understood the struggle for social justice to be a spiritual struggle. Imbedded in his witness, however, are some persistent dilemmas. When does authentic prayer blur into political technique? And a question of integrity and hospitality within a pluralistic society: How to integrate practices specific to one's faith tradition into a social movement, without either watering down one's spirituality or imposing it on people with diverse beliefs and traditions?

Chapter 7

DIVISION IN THE BODY: PRAYER AND ABORTION

———

It was an early Saturday morning in Brookline, Massachusetts. Outside the Planned Parenthood clinic— a large steel and brick building on a busy street— a group of about one hundred protesters gathered. One held up a large sign with a graphic picture and a prolife message. Some distributed pamphlets. Several clustered near the entrance to the clinic, waiting to speak a word to women who entered. Planned Parenthood escorts wearing blue vests lined the front of the building, and when a young woman and man approached they quickly shielded the couple from protestors and ushered them to the entrance. As they neared the door, a woman called out to them not to abort their baby, that they could find help. The door closed behind the couple and the escorts resumed their places.

An above-ground subway rumbled along the street as a middle-aged man holding a microphone led the protestors in reciting the rosary: "Hail Mary, full of grace, the Lord is with thee. Blessed art thou amongst women and blessed is the fruit of thy womb Jesus." The words of the prayer rang out again and again, ten times, followed by the "Glory Be" and the "Our Father." After a while, silence took over. Then the protesters sang a familiar hymn: "Amazing Grace."

A group of Catholic schoolchildren arrived and took their place with the prolife group, praying and holding up a banner that quoted a verse from the Book of Jeremiah: "From my mother's womb the Lord called me by name." As they prayed, some protesters jostled for position with prochoice demonstrators, trying to hold up their own signs in front of the others'. A prolife demonstrator lifted a large wood crucifix. A nun sought to speak with an escort, who repeatedly told her, "No thank you." One young man kneeled on the cement sidewalk in front of the entrance to the clinic. There, amid this most controversial and divisive issue, prayer was right at the front lines.

Does prayer belong in this contentious place? The issue of abortion is painful, personal, political, and divisive. Many of us have strong feelings about this issue. Perhaps we have experienced an unplanned pregnancy in our own family. We may have helped to counsel a friend or colleague. Some of our faith communities have taken a strong stand on abortion. Perhaps abortion was a key question that swayed our vote in a national or local election. For people on all sides of this issue, what is at stake is enormously important. People who call themselves prolife see their commitment as a struggle to protect vulnerable lives and uphold the sacred worth of all life, no matter how small or unseen. People who call themselves prochoice see abortion rights as a key step in the fight for women's equality and health. They point to the oppression and victimization of women and to the complexity of women's lives, asserting that women's difficult decisions regarding abortion must be respected. As positions harden and slogans replace thoughtful dialogue, abortion stirs up divisions that seem unbridgeable. Prayer rings out through it all.

Two Views of Justice

Tom Davis is a United Church of Christ minister and a leading voice of the clergy in the prochoice movement. He has worked with Planned Parenthood for decades, from grassroots clergy organizing to chairing the organization's national Clergy Advisory Board. Before that, he was active in the civil rights movement. He relates how he was drawn to the prochoice movement: as a college chaplain and religion teacher in the mid-1960s, he was approached by students who were concerned about a classmate in their dorm. She was pregnant, afraid to tell her parents, and planning to fly to Puerto Rico for an abortion. Abortion was illegal in the United States at the time. Davis describes feeling completely at a loss. He did not know how to advise the student. He asked a physician at the college to join him in talking with the student.

Davis was struck by the nonjudgmental, empathic words the doctor spoke to the young woman: "We know that the lives of women are very complicated." Davis suddenly understood better what he describes as "the impossible struggle that women faced and still face when it comes to controlling their bodies and their lives." The woman eventually did tell her family, who paid for an abortion in some undisclosed location.[1]

Davis came to see the prochoice movement as an extension of the civil rights movement. He and his wife, Betsy, also a minister, worked actively to help women gain access to abortion. Before abortion was legalized, they were part of a network of clergy across the country that referred women to places where they could get illegal abortions. He describes abortion at that time as both commonplace and "often unsafe, especially for poor women." After the 1973 *Roe* v. *Wade* U.S. Supreme Court decision legalizing abortion, Davis and his wife worked to defend women's right to abortion and give the prochoice movement visible clergy support. In the late 1980s, for example, churches began picketing Saratoga Hospital in upstate New York because it provided abortions. Davis helped to organize a group of local clergy to publicly back the hospital's policy. He believes that women continue to be marginalized, and that their rights are at risk of being subordinated to concern for the fetus. He believes that the prochoice movement is engaged in the "sacred work . . . of securing reproductive justice for women."[2]

Mary Therese Weyrich is a mother who says she has "the heart of a mother." She goes each week to a local abortion clinic and prays quietly for hours outside. "Why do I go there? It is because I *must*. . . . I've been through labor (aptly named) and delivery. I've held that new little baby, looked in his eyes. . . . That is why. Each baby is as precious as my own." As she stands outside the clinic, Weyrich watches with great sadness: "Girls go in scared and come out hurt and crying. I see men waiting around outside, time crawling, their eyes ashamed. I see the staff act as if everything is OK. It is not OK." She says that she prays quietly, never shouting. She pleads to God: "Dear Lord, that this one would stop. No more killing. Please touch the hearts of . . . the workers, the doctors. Please, Lord, that they would find some other work." In her view, ending abortion is a clear matter of justice. She prays outside the clinic because in this place "innocent blood is shed."[3]

It is one thing to talk about praying for peace and justice. But when it comes to saying what constitutes "justice" as relates to abortion, things grow divisive. The *Roe v. Wade* decision declared that a "right of personal privacy" exists under the U.S. Constitution and that the right of privacy encompasses a woman's decision about whether to terminate a pregnancy. Clearly, the court's decision did not resolve but rather served as a lightning rod for debate about justice and abortion. Prolife and prochoice groups subsequently have marked the anniversary of the court decision with protests, rallies, and prayers. For those who seek to "do justice, and to love kindness, and to walk humbly" with their God (Micah 6:8), how do we pray about abortion?

MARKING AN ANNIVERSARY:
LAMENT AND CELEBRATION

They filled the stadium—high school students, grade school children, college kids, thousands and thousands of them. Decked in jeans and Catholic school uniforms, they wore T-shirts with slogans ("Defend Life," "Abortion Is Mean," and, in the words of the Dr. Seuss character Horton the Elephant, "A person is a person no matter how small"). The kids started a wave, rising in sections throughout the stadium as a Christian band played and the buzz grew louder. The MCI sports center in Washington, D.C., was overflowing on this anniversary of the *Roe* v. *Wade* decision. Later in the day, thousands would gather for the annual March for Life, a demonstration and walk to the national Capitol to protest the legalization of abortion.

As groups searched for seating, the speaker asked for a moment of stillness, and then the Youth Mass began. Line after line, a procession of bishops and priests entered the stadium while the crowd sang "We have come to the house of the Lord giving praise to the One we adore. . . . We believe that He reigns and His mercy will sustain Our life and breath."[4] Cardinal McCarrick, the archbishop of Washington, led the liturgy. It was a time for the community to come together, give voice to its convictions, lift up the prolife cause in prayer, lament, repent, and send off the spirit-filled crowds to the afternoon march to the Capitol.

In his homily, the Reverend Gerard Francik refused to cede the word *choice* to the prochoice movement. The

Scriptures, he said, are all about choices. The book of Deuteronomy, for example, presents the choices of life and death, blessing and curse. In other biblical texts are found these contrasts: dark, light; anxiety, calm; just, unjust; gracious, obnoxious. The loving God gives us free will, and we are to make loving, good choices. The priest broke into Spanish as he pointed to a cloth image of Our Lady of Guadalupe centrally positioned on the stage. She who sent Juan Diego off to the bishop's palace, she who bolstered him with courage and gave him a sign to convince the powers, said the priest, she will lead us: "Our Lady goes with us, as she did with St. Juan Diego, today to the White House, to Capitol Hill, yes, even to the Supreme Court . . . to say listen to us, make a good choice—choose life!"[5]

The Prayer of the Faithful followed. Young people alternated reading the prayers in nine languages: "For the protection of all human life throughout the world. For an end to terrorism, war, abortion, infanticide, capital punishment, assisted suicide, euthanasia, child abuse, human cloning, embryonic stem cell research, and all forms of violence in our land. . . . That the motherhood of Mary may be an inspiration to all Christians to see every life as a gift from God that must be protected and nurtured in His love. . . . For healing of all those wounded by abortion. . . . Let us pray to the Lord."

After Communion, the recessional hymn "Go Make a Difference" concluded the Mass. With police escort, the youths poured out onto 7th Street, where they walked with banners and music and cheering down to Constitution Avenue to join the March for Life. They walked side by side, Baptists and Lutherans, evangelicals and groups not religiously affiliated. Several hours later, politicians and religious leaders greeted the marchers with speeches on the steps of the Capitol. President Bush phoned in a supportive message.

On January 22, 2003, worshippers gathered in another Washington, D.C., spot to mark the anniversary of *Roe* v. *Wade*—here, though, in prayerful celebration. In the New York Avenue Presbyterian Church, led by an interfaith team of Christian, Jewish, Buddhist, and Ethical Humanist prayer leaders, worshippers gave thanks for thirty years of legal abortion and for all those who have worked to protect women's right to choose to terminate a pregnancy: "We are gathered here to honor the heroic women and men who labored and sacrificed to liberate women from the chains of misguided patriarchalism." The service was a kind of rally, affirming the cause as a struggle for justice, seeking strength for the work ahead. Those gathered lifted up prayers for women, children, men, families, abortion providers, and government leaders—prayers that alluded to the complexity and agony of women's life situations. For women with problem pregnancies: "We pray for women who know that life is beginning within them, who face the agony of wondering what to do in difficult circumstances. . . . The reasons for their dilemmas are as varied as the women themselves. None of us can walk in their shoes. . . . Help them, Gracious God, to find wise counsel, an understanding friend, and caring and compassionate clergy."

The people also somberly remembered those who had died—women who lost their lives seeking illegal and unsafe abortions, abortion providers killed for their work. Candles were lit as each name rang out: "Dr. David Gunn

... Lt. Col. James Barrett ... Leanne Nichols ... Shannon Lowney ... Officer 'Sandy' Sanderson ... Dr. Barnett Slepian." The people prayed: "Help us, Gracious God, to stand together with these courageous and caring people who continue to do your holy work."

The worshippers refused to surrender the term *life* to those in the prolife movement. Rather, they affirmed the mystery of life as they called on God, "Creator of us all," to stand with those gathered. Rabbi Marc Israel read, from the book of Deuteronomy, the same passage referred to in the Youth Mass for Life: "I have set before you life and death, blessings and curses. Choose life so that you and your descendants may live" (30:19). In response to prayers for women who are victims of violence, for families struggling to nurture the children they already have, for pregnant teenage girls who may not see that they have a future of their own, the leader called out "As we bless the source of life," and the people responded: "So are we blessed." The service included a collection for the National Network of Abortion Funds, which gives financial assistance to thousands of women seeking abortions each year.[6]

The "Sacred Work" of Defending Women's Right to Abortion: Prochoice Clergy Speak Up

The Religious Coalition for Reproductive Choice organized this worship service at New York Avenue Presbyterian Church in commemoration of *Roe* v. *Wade.* At the same time, it marked its own thirtieth anniversary; the organization began in the wake of the 1973 Supreme Court decision as an alliance of Protestant and Jewish groups forming the Religious Coalition for Abortion Rights. Their mission: to preserve women's legal right to an abortion against all foes, including the religious prolife movement. Today the group calls itself the Religious Coalition for Reproductive Choice. They encourage people of faith to take action politically to defend abortion rights.

If religion typically is seen as sitting squarely in the prolife camp, such groups represent another side of the story. Organizations such as Planned Parenthood, the largest contemporary provider of abortion services in the United States, are stepping up efforts to show religious support for their work. Planned Parenthood advocates strongly for abortion rights and runs centers that offer abortion, contraception, and health services around the world. Recently it has worked to reinvigorate and develop alliances with clergy and religious congregations. Planned Parenthood began a Church Partnership program and even staffs clinics in some churches. The organization publishes a journal called "Clergy Voices." It sponsors an annual interfaith prayer breakfast. Planned Parenthood, which is not religiously affiliated, even hired a national chaplain.

The Reverend Ignacio Castuera, a United Methodist minister, became the first national chaplain of Planned Parenthood in 2004. He came to the position with extensive experience in local pastoral ministry and church leadership, the first Mexican American district superintendent of the Los Angeles district of United Methodist churches. He also brought a history of fervent support for what he describes as "sexual and reproductive freedom for women," having served on the board of the Los Angeles Planned Parenthood chapter and worked in outreach to the Latina community. Castuera sees abortion rights as essential, particularly for poor women who could not otherwise afford the procedure: "So choice is related to income and social location and color in America," he said. He passionately links the prochoice movement with his faith: "The prochoice movement is in complete alliance with the prophetic movement of Israel and with the gospel message of Jesus of Galilee."[7]

Castuera thought long and hard about accepting the position as chaplain. He describes this time as prayer—"sorting things out in front of God." He also sees prayer as being his entire walk with God; prayer can be a moment when one is more aware of one's communication with God, but it also happens integrally as we live our lives. So, understanding his life and work as prayer, he talked with his family, especially his three daughters. He believed strongly in the prochoice cause and also feared that as a high-profile prochoice religious leader he could be the target of violence. He shared his thoughts and feelings and, with his daughters' support, decided to accept the position. As chaplain, he believes that he is a "symbol, a living reminder of the close relationship between progressive religious forces and the struggle for sexual and reproductive freedom for women." Like Tom Davis, he calls the work of Planned Parenthood "sacred work." As chaplain, Castuera works with communities of faith to build networks of support for Planned Parenthood's mission and activities.

Division in the Body

Castuera sharply condemns the prolife movement and its public prayer, which he calls "ranting and raving and grand-standing." Castuera argues: "The pro-life movement completely defies the teachings of Jesus because it uses prayer in direct opposition to the directives of Jesus." To back up his statement, he refers to Jesus' words in the gospel of Matthew: "And whenever you pray, do not be like the hypocrites; for they love to stand and pray in the synagogues and at the street corners, so that they may be seen by others. Truly I tell you, they have received their reward. But whenever you pray, go into your room and shut the door and pray to your Father who is in secret; and your Father who sees in secret will reward you" (Matthew 6:5–6). For Castuera, this text offers a clear warning about the dangers of public prayer, which should be kept to a minimum, he says. Prayer is an intimate, quiet relationship with God, who is trusted friend, lover, and parent. One should not call attention to oneself in prayer. In contrast to prolife prayer, he says, prochoice prayer is "non-theatrical."[8]

PRAYER OUTSIDE THE CLINICS: SOLIDARITY AND SPIRITUAL WARFARE

For those who oppose abortion, however, the stakes are too high to pray quietly behind closed doors. Prayer needs to be taken to the streets and to the seats of power. Prayer needs to happen where abortion happens. For some prolife supporters, praying outside an abortion clinic expresses solidarity—and even an actual relationship—with the unborn. ("We recognize them as our brothers and sisters, welcoming them into the human family. We embrace them, spiritually," writes one pro-life group.) They compare prayer in front of an abortion clinic to a bedside prayer vigil in a hospital with a loved one: "When our loved ones lay dying in intensive care units, we keep constant watch. Many prayers are said outside the dying person's room. Even Jesus did not want to be alone before he died."[9] Those who gather in the public spaces in front of clinics pray for the unborn, marking what is happening inside the clinic, that it not go unnoticed. They witness to their belief that the fetus is indeed a person, a child of God, facing its death. There is a sense of the church underlying this prayer; the fetus is regarded as a spiritual brother or sister—one of the saints—who should be recognized, loved, and mourned. Prayer affirms the connectedness of all life.

Prochoice advocates, by contrast, likely would see this practice as offensive, a way of thrusting one's viewpoint about when life begins into the faces of women confronting an agonizing decision. Prochoice supporters also want to extend solidarity to the oppressed, but they would differ on who the victims in the abortion controversy are. With whom should we express our solidarity in prayer? For many in the prochoice movement, the victims are women in a vulnerable position who need support, not harassment from sidewalk counselors; women whose access to abortion lies under threat; and abortion providers who face physical danger in their work—at the hands of some of the very people who call themselves prolife.

Division in the Body

Still, prolife demonstrators are unlikely to keep their prayer behind closed doors. Many believe that abortion calls for spiritual conversion, and public prayer is an important part of that process. As a Chicago bishop who joined hundreds of people to pray in the rain outside a Chicago abortion clinic put it: "Maybe it's time we faced up to it—prayer is about the only way left to change people's hearts on this issue."[10]

Indeed, some opponents of abortion see themselves engaged in spiritual warfare, with prayer right on the front lines. The group Helpers of God's Precious Infants describes their vigils outside abortion clinics: "The Pray-ers come to the abortion mill for an hour or more on any morning that the babies are going to be killed. They carry on a most important spiritual battle as they stand outside the mill." In their words, they love the people but hate what they are doing. Through their sacrifice and prayers, they seek to change the hearts of women entering the clinic. They also support with prayer the group's "sidewalk counselors," who directly approach women and their partners to try to persuade them not to have an abortion.[11]

The fight against abortion is, for some, a real confrontation with evil, for which prayer is an essential weapon. The biblical letter to the Ephesians expresses this sense of spiritual battle: "Put on the whole armor of God, so that you may be able to stand against the wiles of the devil. . . . Stand therefore, and fasten the belt of truth around your waist, and put on the breastplate of righteousness." Paradoxically, part of the armor for battle is the gospel of peace, with faith as a shield and the Word of God as a sword: "As shoes for your feet put on whatever will make you ready to proclaim the gospel of peace. . . . With all of these, take the shield of faith, with which you will be able to quench all the flaming arrows of the evil one. Take the helmet of salvation, and the sword of the Spirit, which is the word of God" (Ephesians 6:11–17). The very next line of the text, following right on the heels of this battle imagery, is the counsel to "pray in the Spirit at all times" (6:18).

This same sense of urgency and danger informs the work of some prolife groups. Priests for Life explain: "Some activists, in praying at abortion mills, rightly acknowledge that we must pray against evil spirits, who are very real and very active to keep abortion going."[12] Prayer then seeks to wrestle evil for the hearts of women, their partners, clinic workers, legislators, and all those involved with the provision of abortion. Is this theatrics or witness? What makes some public practices of prayer prophetic and others "ranting and raving"?

PRAYER AS WITNESS: A PROLIFE PILGRIMAGE

It would be difficult to miss the message on the T-shirts. In large blue letters on a white background, the words *PRO-LIFE* are unmistakable. Every person in the group walking across the Golden Gate Bridge wears the shirt; it is, as they say, their "habit." The young adults are setting out on a thirty-two-hundred-mile trek across the country to Washington, D.C. They walk in shifts, praying individually

Division in the Body

and together at frequent celebrations of the Mass, stopping on weekends to speak in local churches and to pray outside abortion clinics. Like those on the March for Life, they see their walk as an important public witness, a journey to restore a "culture of life" in "witnessing to the dignity and sanctity of all human life from the moment of conception to natural death." It is, they say, a pilgrimage. The organization that sponsors the walk, Crossroads, was founded in 1994 by a college student seeking to give young adults a role in fostering a prolife culture in the United States. It is a Roman Catholic group open to all Christians who wish to support its mission. The organization explains the aim of the cross-country walk: "During our pilgrimage across the United States, we strive always to join our efforts, prayers, and small sacrifices with the sufferings of Christ Crucified for the sake of the innocent. Part of the mission of our walk is to speak to the survivors of abortion—the youth of America."[13]

Sarah Vyvlecka is an eighteen-year-old from Nebraska and a freshman majoring in philosophy. She decided to undertake the walk "simply because of my sincere love of the pro-life movement, and the opportunity Crossroads provides to spend the summer completely immersed in a pro-life mission based on prayer and sacrifice. . . . I pray that our witness touches the lives of all we encounter." Jonathan Teichert, a college senior, hoped to bring the pro-life message across America: "I became involved in the pro-life movement by praying in front of the Planned Parenthood in Ventura, California. Crossroads presents a real opportunity to do more than praying and witnessing for an hour a week in the sleepy corner of Ventura; it is a chance to carry the pro-life message across the nation and to constantly pray for the unborn." Miles Foley, nineteen, is convinced that prayer makes a difference: "I know our sacrifice and prayer really does change the hearts and minds of those we come in contact with."[14] These prolife pilgrims, then, embark in a spirit of prayer, penitential sacrifice, peaceful witness, adventure, and an optimistic sense of making a difference. After three months of walking, they complete their journey on their knees on the steps of the U.S. Supreme Court.

POLARIZED PRAYERS

It was a cold January day as people filed into the Cathedral of St. John the Divine in New York City. Pews were filled with those who had known and loved Shannon Lowney and Leanne Nichols, with those who were simply horrified by their violent deaths. Shannon Lowney was twenty-five, a recent honors graduate of Boston College working as a receptionist in a Planned Parenthood clinic in Brookline, Massachusetts. Leanne Nichols was thirty-eight, an office worker at another abortion clinic nearby. On December 30, 1994, antiabortion extremist John Salvi walked into the Planned Parenthood clinic, spraying it with gunfire. Shannon Lowney died. Salvi then went down the street to another clinic and killed Nichols. Five others were wounded in the attacks. It was not the first shocking experience of violence. The Brookline attacks followed on the heels of several other murders. In 1993, a religious prolife advocate took a gun out in the parking lot of a clinic in Pensacola, Florida, and killed Dr. David Gunn, a physician who performed abortions at the clinic. The following year, an activist named Paul Hill, a defrocked Presbyterian minister, went to the same clinic and shot dead another physician and an escort. The threat of violence pressed in on the prochoice movement.

On that January day, then, hundreds of people gathered to memorialize Shannon Lowney and Leanne Nichols, grieve, and renew the commitment and personal bonds of the prochoice movement. Religious leaders from a number of traditions—the dean of the cathedral, a prominent rabbi, the head of the National Council of Churches of Christ in the USA, a Unitarian Universalist leader— came together to lead the worship. This prayer, written by Episcopal priest Rev. G. Anthony Hoeltzel, was read during the service:

> O God,
> You are known by many names
> And your people hear your will spoken in many
>   different ways—
> but most clearly you are known by the
> names of Justice, Freedom, and Peace. . . .
> You have given some among us the special gifts of
>   healing—physicians, nurses,
> and aides; clinic staff and volunteers.
> Yet some would deny these Your servants the right to
>   exercise their gifts as
> they and You have determined best for us.
> Some would deny it by intimidation, some by
>   obstruction,
> And some, Lord, by terror, violence, or even death.

LORD, HAVE MERCY

We ask your special blessing this day, O God, upon
 those whose commitment to
providing your children all the choices you have
 given us has placed them
under attack, and who labor daily under the most
 difficult and terrifying
circumstances to deliver quality health care.[15]

Though many in the prolife movement lamented the murders of Lowney and Nichols, they would see this prayer as heresy. Has God given us the choice to abort? Would God bless the labor of those who provide abortions? Very different views are woven into the prayers published by Priests for Life on its Website and in the liturgical resources sent weekly to clergy. These prayers are infused with a spirit of repentance and resolve. For example, a litany written by director and Catholic priest Rev. Frank Pavone calls repeatedly for God's mercy in the face of "the sin of abortion," the "exploitation of women by abortion," the "silence of Your people." All are encouraged to pray daily for the end of abortion and to devote themselves wholeheartedly to action on behalf of the cause, not as a "hobby to be squeezed in when we have time, but as the very heart and soul of our quest for justice in this world. . . . Prayer is the foundation of all we do in the pro-life movement," explains Rev. Pavone.[16]

Those gathered at the Cathedral of St. John the Divine marked the deaths of Shannon Lowney and Leanne Nichols by praying for courage among those who work in abortion services; Priests for Life pray that those same abortion providers will repent and desist from this work. The group publishes a series of meditations to be used in the "stations of the cross," a traditional Catholic devotion that involves prayer before fourteen images (stations) that portray Jesus' Passion. Pausing before the sixth station, an image of Veronica wiping the face of Jesus as he carries the cross, one is encouraged to offer this prayer: "The compassion Veronica shows reflects the compassion of so many medical doctors and nurses, who treat their patients with dignity. We pray for repentance and renewal in the medical profession. May the tools and skills meant for healing nevermore be used for killing."[17] Does God bless those who work to provide abortion under threatening circumstances, or is the practice of abortion a distorted misuse of the gifts God has given? Should we ask God to give abortion workers courage, or conversion?

The Religious Coalition for Reproductive Choice also posts prayers on its Website—prayers for pregnant women, prayers for foster mothers, prayers for men, prayers for immigrant women. The prayer for "Providers of Women's Health Care" thanks God, the "Gracious Provider of Care and Protection," for doctors, nurses, and other health care workers who train women to use contraception, who educate youth about sexuality, who counsel pregnant women, and who support women through the experience of abortion. The prayer includes a moment of silence for health care providers who have been violently attacked: "We pray for an end to the rhetoric and violent acts that target health care providers, and pray for the day when health care providers, women and their families, can exercise their rights to reproductive choice in security and peace." It closes by echoing the words from the *Roe* v. *Wade* anniversary service, extolling the work of all professionals involved in provision of abortion: "Help us, Gracious God, to stand together with these courageous and caring people who continue to do your holy work."[18]

Like the Religious Coalition for Reproductive Choice, Priests for Life also understands God as a God of care and protection. They pray to God as "Father of all Life"; they praise God "for the Fatherly care which You extend to all creation." The question is, Whom must God protect? Those who oppose abortion cannot fathom a God whose care and protection would not extend to the fetus. They ask God to "extend Your hand of protection to those threatened by abortion, and save them from its destructive power."[19] One group calls abortion holy work; the other denounces it as destructive power. How can these groups name God in such similar ways, yet arrive at such very different conclusions about how God cares for and protects creation? Is one prayer grounded in truth and the other in falsehood?

BROKENNESS IN THE BODY

Kathleen Buckley was a Protestant chaplain at two colleges in upstate New York. One January morning, she stood outside a Planned Parenthood clinic with three other Protestant ministers escorting women into the clinic. Also outside the clinic were a nun and a priest, kneeling in prayer. Several times that morning, the Protestant ministers prayed aloud at the same time as the nun and the priest:

And whenever they would come to the "Our Father" we would join our voice as one. It was a very powerful experience for me. . . . I felt moved by the experience, and yet I am at a loss as I try to communicate to you how I felt. It was at the very least a mix of feelings: sad and angry and grateful. Praying together, using the very same words and yet the way we live those words out couldn't be further apart. It was an odd sense of sharing a core connection to God that is somehow severed at a very basic level. Bleeding and whole at the same time? It was a day I won't soon forget.[20]

The letter to the Ephesians exhorts the young Christian community to live humbly together in love, "with all humility and gentleness, with patience, bearing with one another in love." The body is one, just as there is one Spirit, one Lord, one faith, one baptism. This oneness is integral to the nature of the church. Thus, the letter pleads, make "every effort to maintain the unity of the Spirit in the bond of peace" (Ephesians 4:1–5). How might these words speak across the centuries to Christians wrestling with abortion today, divided at the very place where the one Spirit should guide: in their prayer?

The prayers of prolife and prochoice advocates reveal staggering differences in how people of faith understand human life, God's creation, human freedom, and justice. They show the danger of deceiving ourselves—how easily we can wrap our convictions in prayer, lifting up falsehoods to God, turning worship into a rally. In the abortion debate, each side might accuse the other of doing just that. How, then, do we discern authentic, true prayer?

It seems that we must be able to pray our convictions, if prayer is to be heartfelt and genuine. Yet especially when dealing with public prayer about such a critical issue, there is also a place for saying no to prayer that seems false and misleading. In some ways, this is disturbing; most of us do not like our communication with God to be judged. Still, particularly because many in the abortion debate quite visibly claim a Christian identity, we have to ask whether Christians gathered in a public way to pray are naming God and God's purposes in the world faithfully. Moreover, how do we move toward healing in the Body? How do we pray with love, united in the same Spirit, when the stakes of our differences are as high as life and death?

Chapter 8

GOING TO THE WELLSPRINGS OF TRUST: THE TAIZÉ VISION

―――――

The Burgundy vineyards stretch out into the distance, a scene of gently rolling hills and open sky. A bell clangs and young people stream toward the Taizé Church of Reconciliation, a large, rectangular building, nondescript from the outside but glowing with candles and icons inside. The youths, most of whom are between fifteen and thirty years old, fill the sides and back of the church. Lining the center area are the Taizé brothers, some eighty men, uniform in their white robes but ranging from dark-haired to white-haired. At the rear sits Brother Roger, who founded the community in the 1940s. Much has changed since those early days. A number now flashes onto an electronic screen and the assembled open their songbooks. Strains of "Laudate Omnes Gentes, Laudate Dominum" (number twenty-three) fill the air, over and over again. A young man in jeans and a sweatshirt kneels and closes his eyes. Teenagers in sweatshirts look around, some singing, some whispering to a neighbor. Evening prayer has begun.

Taizé is an ecumenical and international community located in the village of that name in southeastern France. It is a village so small one could easily drive through it en route to Cluny or Dijon without noticing that it had slipped by in the distance. Founded during World War II, the Taizé community from its origins understood itself to be a contemplative community and—in its life as a praying community composed of Protestants and Catholics of many nationalities—a quiet witness for peace and reconciliation. This is a spiritual setting far removed from contentious debate over abortion, from the urgent struggle against apartheid, from public marches to political centers. The Taizé testimony rings out as clear as the bell on the Church of Reconciliation; prayer itself is our mission. The community does not pray for the sake of a social or political end; the prayer itself is the witness and center of Christian life. At the same time, they believe that contemplation does bear fruit in forging bonds of trust among people.

I went to Taizé hoping, like so many of its visitors, to slow down, to find there a deep experience of God. I felt stress melt away as I entered the large church, breathed in the scent of incense, rested in the silence. I felt I was gravitating to a center there. What did this experience, though, have to do with ordinary life? Did it have anything to do with war, or AIDS, or immigration, or poverty? Was I retreating into a world that was simpler, stiller, than the world I read about in the newspaper that morning?

Here we could sing chants containing beautiful images of light and peace, chants that had few words, repeated many times in simple melodies. Here we could kneel in silent contemplation. Here we could feel communion, among hundreds of fellow seekers, an enormous international community, all singing the same words, living in the same quarters for a week, before we went on our way. How real was this communion? Would those few words of promise sustain us once our lives blended back into the realities reflected in the newspaper?

My trip to Taizé raises a problem many Christians wrestle with: How do those contemplative moments of prayer that are so important to sustaining our spirit relate to action in the world? We do not want prayer to be a retreat in the sense of withdrawal from concern about our world. How does prayer change us in a way that yields fruit in our relationships? How to bring contemplation and action together?

THE LIFE OF PRAYER AT TAIZÉ

For Roger Schutz (1915–2005), the founder of Taizé, prayer was the ground of reconciliation. His vision was forged in the midst of World War II. In 1940, Schutz traveled from Switzerland to France. The son of a Swiss father and a French mother, and a Protestant, he studied theology at Lausanne and Strasbourg. He described his sense of calling during the war: "I found myself as if impelled to do everything I could to build a community life in which reconciliation would be realized, made concrete, day by day. To begin with I must start a life of

Going to the Wellsprings of Trust

prayer alone. I would find a house where there would be prayer in the morning, at midday and in the evening and I would take those who were fleeing, those in hiding."[1] Schutz visited the small village of Taizé, which was located near the border between free and occupied France.[2] He bought a house in the village and began to offer shelter to war refugees, including Jews fleeing the Nazis. Two other young men joined him, and a fledgling community life took shape. However, in 1942 the Nazis overtook all of France and—in danger—Schutz left Taizé and went to Geneva. After the liberation of France in 1944, he returned with a small group of brothers. Aided by Schutz's sister Genevieve, the community cared for orphans left adrift from the war. Gradually, the community took shape.

Today the community is composed of about one hundred Protestant and Roman Catholic brothers from several nations. Taizé sees itself as "a concrete sign of reconciliation between divided Christians and separated peoples." The brothers take vows of celibacy, community of material and spiritual goods, adherence to the direction of the prior, and care for fellow brothers.[3] Small groups of brothers live elsewhere, in poor neighborhoods on several continents—in Bahia, Brazil; the Hell's Kitchen neighborhood on the West Side of Manhattan; Dakar, Senegal; and Seoul, Korea. They are on mission, a witness in these regions, but they return regularly to Taizé and remain in communion with the brothers and the prior there.

Theirs is a quiet witness. The brothers avoid taking any visible political stand; rather, they practice a simple witness of presence. They aim to build trust and friendship through personal relationships. In 1962 brothers began to visit young Christians behind the Iron Curtain. Over the next twenty-seven years, those visits increased as they developed friendships in many countries of Central and Eastern Europe. Brother Roger himself traveled to Russia in 1978 and 1988. Following one of these trips, the Taizé community donated one million copies of the New Testament, translated into Russian, for distribution in cities such as Moscow, Leningrad, and Kiev. The prayer of the community has been deeply influenced by these ties to Russia. At the request of Russian Orthodox Christians, the brothers began praying around an icon of the cross; this prayer remains the center of worship on Friday evenings at Taizé.[4]

Today the community attracts thousands of young people each year, peaking in the summer months. Most come for a week at a time, camping in tents and basic dormitory housing. They gather several times each day for communal prayer and meet in groups for cross-cultural discovery and discussion of spiritual issues. They participate in Bible study and choir practice. They pitch in to cook and serve food, wash the dishes, and clean the bathrooms. They also spend time just hanging out, congregating at the snack bar, playing music or tossing a ball around in the fields, walking around the nearby towns, hitching a ride somewhere. It is a scene that is part religious revival, part hippie fun, part earnest seeking, part quiet yearning.

At the Church of the Reconciliation in present-day Taizé, communal prayer happens three times a day. The young visitors fill the hall, surrounding the monks who pray in the center. Prayer is central to the life of the community, and music is integral to the prayer. Crafted and honed over many years, the distinctive Taizé music consists of short, simple chants, translated and sung in several languages, among them Latin, French, Spanish, German, English, Russian, and Polish. Simple repetitive chants express the faith in easily graspable ways, without, as Brother Roger put it, overintellectualizing or "smothering" the mystery of God with too many words.[5] The introduction to the Taizé songbook explains: "Using just a few words, they [the chants] express a basic reality of faith, quickly grasped by the mind. As the words are sung over many times, this reality gradually penetrates the whole being."[6] In this way, Taizé music picks up the long Christian tradition of *lectio divina,* as Brother Roger notes: "For many Christians down through the ages, a few words repeated endlessly have been a road to contemplation."[7]

Lectio divina literally means holy or divine reading. It is an ancient Christian practice of slowly, prayerfully reading the Bible so that it becomes part of your life. Benedict's *Rule,* for example, counseled monks to take time each day for holy reading. This reading was part of a balanced life—of work, prayer, study, rest. Over time, the practice of lectio divina gained structure. A medieval writer by the name of Guigo II described it as a fourfold practice of taking in the word of Scripture as if one were eating it. First one reads or hears the Word (lectio). This is like putting food whole in one's mouth. Then, one meditates on the Word—chewing it, ruminating on it (*meditatio*). Third, one prays into the word, turning the heart's desires to God. This is like tasting the flavor of what one eats (*oratio*). Finally, one rests in contemplation, an enjoyment of the lingering sweetness (*contemplatio*).[8]

The Taizé form of prayer adapts the lectio divina practice, including its emphasis on community as the context for prayer, hoping to open the soul to God and to others by focusing and opening us to the Word experienced in song and silent contemplation. As the Taizé songbook explains, "Nothing fosters a communion with God more than a meditative prayer with others, with singing that goes on and on and that continues afterwards in the silence of one's heart." This is not rushed prayer. The repetitive chanting, the silence, invites people to slow down. In a fast-paced, individualistic culture accustomed to news blips and sound bites, this means of praying offers people a way to sit still, talk less, truly give attention, and enter deeply into the Word.

As I close my eyes, the voices blend into a rich, soothing sound, chanting over and over again: "Bless the Lord, my soul, and bless his holy name." I am drawn to join in, and it does not take long to learn the words. This is a song of praise and adoration, holding a promise: bless the Lord, my soul, who leads me into life.

Taizé music holds the promise of the gospel: life in and through the light of Christ. They do not speak much about social justice or a mission in the world. They sing of waiting for the Lord, trusting in Christ, rejoicing in the resurrection. They offer us a way to lift up our hearts to God. "Sing out my soul" exclaims one chant, and "glorify the Lord who sets us free" ("Magnificat" [canon]). The familiar tune "Ubi Caritas" reminds that God is present in love. In God our souls find rest; this is the message of another song.

These are words of good news: God saves us, frees us, loves us, leads us into life. This is the gospel in music.

As I sit in the darkened church, candles flickering all around me, I cannot help but notice that the words we sing also contain many images of darkness and light. One song describes Jesus Christ as the "lumière intérieure," the light within. God kindles a "fire that never dies away" within our darkest night ("Dans Nos Obscurités"). The Lord is a light that "enlightens my darkness" ("C'est toi ma lampe, Seigneur"). The songs invoke the Holy Spirit to "come to us, kindle in us the fire of your love" ("Tui amoris ignem"). We prayed too: "Let not my doubts nor my darkness speak to me" ("Jésus le Christ"). We may be confused, afraid, lonely, doubting, grieving, but the music proclaims that there is a way out of the darkness. Jesus Christ is the light that illumines our path, a light drawing us to life. For Taizé, any social mission flows from that gospel and the effect of prayer on the human person.

CONTEMPLATION AS CHRISTIAN PRACTICE

Through prayer, Taizé seeks to open us up to our innate capacity and desire for contemplative communion with God. The chants are critical. Somehow we let go as we repeat the words over and over again, in multiple languages. We let go of our usual patterns of thought. We let our guard down; we relax and release. We become more ready to be filled. Worship at Taizé also includes a period of silence. This too is an important time. The singing leads into the silence; song yields to the stillness. The song and the silence are both important dimensions of contemplation.

Contemplation is a venerable practice in the Christian tradition. The anonymous fourteenth-century English author of *The Cloud of Unknowing* describes contemplation as sheer yearning for God, whom we can never know through words, reason, or activity. Between us and God lies a dark cloud of unknowing; only love can pierce it. In contemplation we fix our gaze solely on God. The author tells us to "beat upon that thick cloud of unknowing with the dart of your loving desire and do not cease come what may." There, in the darkness, the author tells, God "will bring you to a deep experience of himself."[9] In her autobiography, Teresa of Avila describes a prayer of union, a state of unspeakable delight with God. She invites us to imagine our souls as a garden being watered by abundant rain: "For the Lord waters the garden without any work on our part—and this way is incomparably better than all the others mentioned." This contemplative prayer, a gift from God, leaves the soul incredibly humble and keenly aware of the "world's vanity."[10]

Christian spiritual authors often distinguish contemplation from meditation. The latter involves active use of our faculties (reason, imagination); the former moves beyond thought and language. It is quieter, more restful. To contemplate is to see, to give attention. In French, to attend (*attendre*) means to wait. Contemplation involves a kind of waiting. It is a pause from our striving, a pause from our talking. It is time to listen. The Biblical figure typically pointed to as a contemplative model is Mary of

Going to the Wellsprings of Trust

Bethany, who sat at the Lord's feet and listened to Jesus while her sister Martha ran around doing all the work necessary to welcome Jesus into their home (Luke 10:38–42). Contemplation is a kind of loving rest with God. Here one thinks of the beloved disciple at the Last Supper who reclined next to Jesus (or, as some translations put it, leaned back on Jesus' breast; John 13:23, 25). This image captures the essence of contemplation: an intimacy with God, resting in the heart of divine love.

MARTHA SPEAKS UP

The difficulty, as we explore how prayer flows into and out of a concern for social justice, is whether contemplation draws attention away from action. Is contemplation a retreat from work and responsibility? As her sister sat at Jesus' feet, the busy Martha protested to Jesus, "Lord, do you not care that my sister has left me to do all the work by myself?" (Luke 10:40). Contemplation may be restful, grace-filled communion with God, but how does contemplation solve the world's problems? In apartheid South Africa, for example, would such singular devotion to the practice of contemplation seem like a passive acquiescence to the status quo? Can contemplation be "prophetic prayer"? Faced with the imperative of the struggle, would South African Christians want to turn with Martha to Jesus and say, "Tell her then to help me" (Luke 10:40)?

Of course, Jesus' response to Martha in Luke's gospel is quite familiar: "Martha, Martha, you are worried and distracted by many things; there is need of only one thing. Mary has chosen the better part, which will not be taken away from her" (Luke 10:41). Jesus' response points us to simplicity and purity of heart. We are so often pulled in a thousand directions, running here and there, totally involved in our own activity. We miss the essential. We forget to be still and listen for God's voice.

Unfortunately, in treasuring contemplation, classic Christian spiritual writers too often devalue action in the world. Some see in Jesus' response to Martha an endorsement of the contemplative life as being more perfect than the active life, or even disdain for concerns of this world as distractions to the spiritual life. *The Cloud of Unknowing,* for example, counsels us to put all thoughts about ourselves, others, and anything else of this world below us in a "cloud of forgetting": "You are to concern yourself with no creature whether material or spiritual nor with their situation and doings whether good or ill."[11] Surely this kind of prayer does not encourage social activism or sustained concern for human suffering.

CONTEMPLATION AND ACTION

Is there an innate tension between the contemplative life and our ordinary responsibilities in the world? Let me share a personal story from my own visit to Taizé.

I went to Taizé as a new mother, arriving with my four-month-old baby and my husband. As we walked through an entry room on the way into the Church of the

Reconciliation, I paused, placing my son before a beautiful icon of the Virgin Mary holding the baby Jesus. I felt a kinship with her and some affirmation of the holiness of my new life. Then my eyes drifted upward to a sign right above the icon. "Silence" it read. I wondered at the irony of this sign, posted right above an icon of a baby. Was Mary's baby Jesus quiet? If so, I would have to ask her for some advice.

We went on to the worship, and my son thoroughly enjoyed the chants. Soothing, like a lullaby, the music left him calm in my arms. Once again, I felt affirmed. We could be together in this sacred, contemplative space even as I entered this new vocation of motherhood. The Scripture reading that followed seemed like an unbelievably apt message: "Let the little children come to me, and do not stop them; for it is to such as these that the kingdom of heaven belongs" (Matthew 19:14). As the worship neared the time for silent meditation on the Word, however, I felt a tap on my shoulder. An usher told me that I would need to take my baby out during the silence. I obliged, feeling torn between understanding and resentment. Contemplation requires silence uninterrupted by a child's voice; I understood. I even yearned for the peace and centeredness that a few moments of pure silence bring. Yet how perfectly would a child's babbling bring home a real meditation on that Scripture! How many people are excluded from contemplation because they are not able to free themselves from their work in the world? Is there a way to embrace an intrusion of the world in our contemplation?

The truth, I think, is that every life needs a blend of contemplation and action, two modes of being that ultimately feed each other. Even Teresa of Avila, whose writings focus so much on the interior life, gives us hints about the kind of life that can flow from contemplation. She reminds us that prayer is a gift and that we must be careful to avoid overattachment to the world—a temptation to vanity and distraction. She was keenly aware that "all things pass away; only God endures." This gives a certain perspective that may be healthy and calming for the most active of activists. At the same time, Teresa was not immune from political and social concerns by any means. As I have already noted, she wrote during a dangerous political time. The church was the dominant force in Spain and the Inquisition ruthlessly sought to root out heresy. Her friendship with God sustained her as she critiqued her culture, built a new form of religious life, and negotiated political structures.

How do we put together the beauty of contemplative prayer and our everyday, busy, noisy activities? Do we need to keep each in a separate compartment so to speak, to preserve the purity of the contemplative prayer? I wondered again how Taizé lived out the relationship between contemplative prayer and hospitality, between such prayer and concern for unity and reconciliation.

GOING TO THE
"WELLSPRINGS OF TRUST"

For the Taizé community, a key to understanding how contemplation may yield fruit in society rests in the word *trust*. As one learns to trust God more through prayer, one sees the world differently. Opening oneself to others, as the brothers do through their hospitality, we form bonds of trust and reconciliation with people who may be very different from ourselves. For the Taizé community, "Prayer is not a matter of method or expertise but trust. And to open the doors to trusting in God, there is perhaps nothing to replace the beauty of human voices joined in song."[12] The Holy Spirit strengthens one's capacity to say yes to God's call—a yes that Brother Roger describes as "transparent trust." Trust in God yields a way of seeing the world that is open, perceptive of beauty, discerning, and above all loving. Taizé does not emphasize sin but rather the human capacity to reflect God's presence, respond affirmatively to God's call, bring about "a future of peace and trust." Brother Roger writes to young people that he affirms their "yearning for peace, for communion, and for joy." We human beings have a "spark of goodness in the depths of our soul, a spark which asks only to burst into flame." Through prayerful surrender to God, we can go to those "wellsprings of kindness, of joy, and also to the wellsprings of trust." Therein, we find a way to reflect God's beauty to those whom God has "entrusted" to us. Christ's disciples "are called to be a humble leaven of trust and peace within humanity."[13] In the Taizé vision, through contemplative singing and silence community forms, trust builds among diverse peoples, and a vision of social reconciliation, mutual understanding, and unity grows.

The community seeks to bring this trust to life as it hosts a yearly "pilgrimage of trust on earth" in cities around Europe between Christmas and New Year's. The community estimates that tens of thousands of young people from Europe and beyond participate in these meetings, which have taken place every year since 1978. Young people stay with host families or in local churches. During the five days, the young people all pray together in city centers, as well as meeting in small groups in the neighborhoods where they are staying. The meetings are intended to promote cross-cultural understanding and discovery, common experiences of prayer and silence, group sharing, and spiritual reflection. The result is "to weave threads of trust."[14]

Here is how one of the young people who participated in a pilgrimage of trust in Paris described his experience. He was surprised, he said, to experience the spirit of Taizé—or better, the Holy Spirit—in the midst of a city. What an amazing feeling, to live for five days with two or three dozen other young people from other cultures and yet still experience this fundamental commonality and fullness. He wrote: "It is good to be able to feel that we can be together, sitting on the floor, singing beautiful songs that fill us up inside, as if we needed nothing else to live from."[15] Would the experience help him shape and nurture community when he returned to his regular life? Would he participate in a faith community at home? Or does Taizé offer a short-term, peak experience of prayer and community that has little lasting impact, an experience that is separated from the ongoing life of congregation and local community?

Even the short-term experience of trust and simple joy that many find at Taizé is vulnerable, as the community discovered one Tuesday evening in August 2005. The events of that evening contradict any thought that contemplation shields one from the real world. While twenty-five hundred people prayed in the Church of the Reconciliation, a thirty-five-year-old woman surged toward Brother Roger and stabbed him three times in the neck. He died within minutes. The founder of this community of prayer, this witness for peace and reconciliation, had been murdered—right in the middle of worship. How could this be? How would the community respond to this shock?

They responded, along with many around the world, with grief and disbelief. Yet they also extended their hands in forgiveness and compassion. The woman who had killed Brother Roger seemed to be mentally ill. At the funeral, Brother Alois, the new leader of the community, prayed for her. Echoing Christ's words on the cross, he asked God to forgive her, for she knew not what she did. Brother Alois also pointed to Brother Roger's kindheartedness, a "vulnerable reality" that is, however, able to "transform the world." At his funeral, the community lifted up Brother Roger's conviction that (in the words of Brother Alois) "God's peace will have the last word for each person on earth."

BRINGING TAIZÉ HOME

When I went to Taizé, I wondered what this contemplative monastic community could teach me about prayer engaged with the world. I had some questions in mind:

Does contemplative prayer deflect attention from action in this world? Is it an example of precisely the vertical focus that allows social injustice to go unchecked? Taizé's answer, I think, is that prayer is the most important action one can take in this world. Only God's peace ultimately will bring peace. Only through prayer do we come to know our own goodness and the love that God has for us. These gifts are essential to all human relations. I imagine that the murder of Brother Roger sorely tested this confidence in human goodness, but the community's response attests to the power that prayer has had in its life.

We are left, then, with a strong witness to the power of contemplative prayer in community. Perhaps the Taizé example invites us to consider whether we have any contemplative space in our own lives. What inner work do we need to do to produce real fruit in the relationships, workplaces, and civic groups in which we participate? What kind of witness might contemplation offer in our own particular communities? We too are left to wonder exactly how the experience of contemplation can be brought home, how the withdrawal in the desert can come full circle to engagement. As we seek to weave together contemplation and action in our own lives, does the Taizé story guide us, or does Martha's voice unsettle us?

Chapter 9

PRAYING WITH CONVICTION AND HUMILITY

—

I can imagine bringing some of the people from these several stories together around a table. I wonder what the conversation would sound like, who would gravitate toward whom, who might argue with whom. Would the South Africans who pushed for a radical, prophetic prayer find the contemplative, politically understated witness of Taizé to be passive? Would members of the Coral Gables congregation hear echoes of their own divisiveness in the even more contentious divide between prolife and prochoice people of faith? I imagine that out of their own struggle toward reconciliation South Africans would have something to say to those conflicted communities, something about how to move toward healing in the body. I picture the farm workers embracing the South African Christians, who, like them, struggled for justice and called out in prayer for radical social transformation. I wonder if prolife supporters would question why they should be criticized for hypocrisy and grandstanding, when they see the groundswell of support enjoyed by the farm workers with their very visible practice of piety. I picture the Taizé brothers sitting quietly in their white robes, listening, open to all, perhaps serving as a reminder to others to stop running long enough, to stop talking long enough, to hear God's voice.

As we imagine such a roundtable, as we think about the stories and the people who fill them, I see an underlying question emerging: What is authentic Christian spirituality? The resounding response that I would offer, shaped by the dialogue with these people of faith, is that life in the Spirit does not entail disengagement from the world but rather careful, prayerful engagement—humble, not presumptuous; prophetic, not passive; yet always contemplative in the best sense. This is not a contemplation that lifts one out of the world to a heavenly vision, leaving behind only disdain for the worldly, but instead a rootedness in God—trusting, attentive, and overflowing to compassion.

The Jesuit theologian Karl Rahner describes prayer as the last moment of speech before the mystery of God draws one to silence and utter self-abandonment: "Prayer can be itself only when it is understood as the last moment of speech before the silence, as the act of self-disposal just before the incomprehensibility of God disposes of one, as the reflexion immediately preceding the act of letting oneself fall, after the last of one's own efforts and full of trust, into the infinite Whole which reflexion can never grasp." It is incredible that one can speak before this transcendent mystery, but God enables one to do so: "*God* is the very possibility of address; he himself brings our prayer about when we pray."[1] Words are possible, and human action has its place; God enables one to bring words and efforts, however limited they might be, before God. Ultimately, though, God's great beyond relativizes all that we say and do. So prayer is not finally a matter of human effort or cleverness in finding the right words. It is speech to God, enabled by God, flowing into silence, awe, and trusting abandonment to God.

Rahner's words bring us back, perhaps, to the spare speech of the desert. We recall that when he was asked how to pray, Abba Macarius responded: "There is no need at all to make long discourses; it is enough to stretch out one's hands and say, 'Lord, as you will, and as you know, have mercy.'" The desert was a place to cultivate silence, and in the silence, discernment. Silence was a difficult but essential spiritual discipline, as this saying conveys: "It was said of Abba Agathon that for three years he lived with a stone in his mouth, until he had learnt to keep silence."[2] In silence one more starkly confronted one's own capacity for self-deception and pride—learning, in a sense, one's true place. It was not that words were unimportant in the desert; rather, they were exceedingly important—both the words that one spoke to God in prayer and the words of discerning counsel to another. When seekers begged for "a word" from the desert elders, the words given were terse and pointed, spoken out of a deep experience of the Spirit.

Jesus too introduced what we today call the Lord's Prayer with an invitation to pray simply, with few words: "When you are praying, do not heap up empty phrases as the Gentiles do, for they think that they will be heard because of their many words. Do not be like them, for

Praying with Conviction and Humility

your Father knows what you need before you ask him" (Matthew 6:7–8). Words heaped on words draw attention to oneself; it becomes self-preoccupying, and possibly performance. The prayer that Jesus taught, on the other hand, is simple and authentic, acknowledging our human need and always placing that need within the larger context of "thy will be done." The Lord's Prayer is humble, but at the same time it is daring in anticipation and hope that God's reign will come.

To discipline our speech is part of the faithful practice of prayer—not in such a way that we truncate our earnest expressions of hope and desire, but so as to open space for the Other and place our desires within the larger context of God's purposes. We are invited to pray simply, humbly, with care for the words we use. At times, silence is the only appropriate prayer.

Nevertheless, the oppression of South Africans, the injustice endured by farm workers, the suffering brought on by war, the pain of women facing difficult pregnancies, the lives of unborn children all call out for response. In the face of suffering, injustice, and tragedy, surely God would not want only our silence. If prayer is indeed the first action that we do for others, as Karl Barth wrote, then we can and must pray on behalf of those whose well-being is affected directly by the policies of government and the quality of society. Sometimes this means praying vocally, publicly, and boldly. The counsel to take care with our words does not mean that Christians are mute in the face of suffering. Rather, there are times when we must pray aloud and with conviction—coupled always with humble, stumbling efforts to find right and true words.

We relinquish neither the call to build up a good society nor the call to stand humbly before a mysterious God whose grace will always exceed the solution we imagine for our situation.

The people who fill the stories in this book, for the most part, do not lack for conviction. They may be an inspiration to those of us who tend to sit on the fence too long, who keep silent when we should speak out, who are immersed in our personal lives and feel little energy for wider political involvement. From Tutu to Chavez, from Pastor Schaper to the many laypeople who seek to make a difference, the people in these stories make a strong case that Christian faith involves engagement with social and political issues; our faith does have something to say about how we vote, how we volunteer, how we pay attention to suffering. In short, what kind of society we build, what injustices we tolerate, matters. At the same time, I come away from the stories more convinced than ever that we need to find ways to couple conviction with greater care for the words we use in public prayer. Too often, prayer is a mouthpiece for a political viewpoint, rather than a space for listening discernment. Too often it conveys certainty with no hint of the mystery of God. Sometimes it is simply false.

Let me share some of my own conviction to illustrate this last point. As I wrote the chapter on abortion, I found it difficult and moving to suspend my own beliefs enough to attempt to convey the meaning of prayer for both pro-life and prochoice advocates. It was an exercise in listening, in empathy. What would it be like to face an anguishing decision about whether to continue a pregnancy? What draws those sidewalk rosary pray-ers to stand out in the cold, creating an atmosphere that others see as harassing? How do some see the prochoice movement as a religious struggle for justice, fully in line with the Hebrew prophets and the ministry of Jesus? On the abortion issue, there is precious little space for this kind of listening, stretching, seeking to understand. I hope that the chapter in some modest way advances more thoughtful, less polarizing dialogue and a movement toward prayerful healing of the deep divisions among us.

At the same time, I found it difficult to leave the questions posed in that chapter completely open-ended, without saying what I believed to be true. Humility and empathy should not paralyze conviction. So, to voice my own belief: I think that some of what we see in this story is not right practice. I simply do not believe, for example, that is it faithful to lift up abortion as "holy work." How can the taking of an innocent life, even under terribly difficult circumstances for the mother, be considered holy or sacred? I can imagine other words that prochoice supporters might lift in prayer: "tragic," "painful," perhaps even "necessary." But holy?

I would like to see more roundtables around which faith communities could gather to openly talk about how to pray, reflect together on the language of their prayer, listen deeply, and even challenge one another in love and for the sake of the church. We hesitate to judge prayer, because prayer is so deeply personal and intimate. But words matter, particularly when we are praying in public, in community. Prayer expresses the identity of the body and shapes the beliefs of those assembled. We are patterned into ways of being through our participation in the prayer of the community. We learn how to use words to address God, how to describe ourselves, how to imagine what God wants for the world, how to act. Do our words in prayer express who we are as the church? Do they form persons of faith well and truly? Do they stand for justice while also leading the community to self-examination, discernment, and healing?

To ask for such careful attention to the language of prayer is a tall order, but one that hopefully will enliven communities in prayer, rather than paralyze them. Ultimately the call for reflection springs from a sense that prayer is indeed powerful and that God has created us with a desire to know God rightly and speak truly even as we pour out our souls to the Creator. Moreover, we find encouragement in the promise given in Paul's letter to the Romans. We do not pray alone; the Holy Spirit is our helper in prayer: "Likewise the Spirit helps us in our weakness; for we do not know how to pray as we ought, but that very Spirit intercedes with sighs too deep for words. And God, who searches the heart, knows what is the mind of the Spirit, because the Spirit intercedes for the saints according to the will of God" (Romans 8:26–27). Even when words fail us—and they will—even when we are blind to what God's will is—and we often are—the Spirit lifts us up according to God's will. We might try to picture the Spirit, a loving counselor and advocate for us, sighing as a parent might sigh on seeing a loved child who needs help. With a deep wordless breath that any parent would recognize, the Spirit asks for what we really need.

The deep wordless sigh of the Spirit then empowers our own stumbling words before God. We can try to pray in ways that are truly attentive to our complex, confusing social and political contexts, always seeking to discern the purposes of God, always cautious about our ability to do so. The stories in this book show the need for continued, careful reflection about how to pray (particularly in public). This is not the place to offer a simple resolution to the dilemmas that arise in the stories; they need to be wrestled with, lived with, as a starting point for searching conversation and prayer. Still, the people who fill these stories also offer some ways forward, some paths into a way of life that is fervently, humbly, and prayerfully engaged with the world. These paths are often surprisingly continuous with well-worn spiritual routes within the Jewish and Christian traditions.

Prayer of Lament

In South Africa, out of decades of oppression arose a prayer of lament—a raw, honest crying out to God for relief. Lament is often a first and entirely authentic response to suffering. The Hebrew Psalms, which have held a central place in the prayer of Christian spiritual guides and communities for centuries, offer a natural resource for this prayer. The psalms put language around both individual and communal experiences of suffering and give us license to question (and even accuse)

God out of that experience. In the South African story, lament merged with political protest, captured visibly in the raised fists of the Cradock mourners. The psalms seem to make space for this merging of prayer and protest. The psalmist too angrily denounces the oppressor; political realities are imbedded in the Israelites' faith experience.

As it questions God and even orders God to take action, lament prayer may not seem too humble. "Rouse yourself! Why do you sleep, O Lord? " (Psalm 44:23) sounds bold if not insolent. Compare this to Rahner's description of awed silence before the incomprehensibility of God. Nonetheless, lament prayer is precisely a mix of conviction and humility. The Israelites are certain that they have been faithful to Yahweh and that God should help them against their enemies. They have not turned away from God, they assert. It is unjust that they are being trounced, humiliated, "scattered like sheep for slaughter." Indeed, they remind God of God's own nature—steadfast and just. Surely, this is a bold prayer. Yet they also know that it is only through God's power that they triumph over their enemies; "Through you we push down our foes. . . . For not in my own bow do I trust, nor can my sword save me" (Psalm 44:5–6). Their awareness of their dependence on God—this posture of utter humility—drives their sharp questioning of God and their prayer for help: "Why do you forget our affliction and oppression? . . . Rise up, come to our help" (Psalm 44:24, 26). In many psalms, the plea for God's "mercy" is a cry—even a demand—that God hear one's prayer and relieve the suffering of God's people.

Prophetic and Discerning Prayer

The Hebrew Scriptures also help to frame prayer that calls for radical, concrete political and social transformation— what some South African leaders called prophetic prayer. When a people persist in sin, when the powers violate God's demand for justice, the prophet is given a word from the Lord to speak. Can one imagine, then, praying in the spirit of the prophets? This would be prayer that lifts up the oppressed, prayer deeply in tune with the God who will not abide the abuse of God's people. Prayer in the spirit of the prophets questions the status quo and confidently calls on God to effect change. It also draws one forward to action to help bring about the just society for which one prays.

Yet the stories in this book should also lead us to affirm an ancient teaching: prophecy must go hand in hand with discernment. Time and again, the Scriptures warn of the dangers of false prophecy. False prophecy is a very real possibility, particularly when one is dealing with the specificity and ambiguity of politics. Prophetic prayer needs to be deeply immersed in a humble practice of seeking more and more to glimpse the will of God for a particular situation. This is not so as to temper the passion for justice but to acknowledge the surprising nature of God's grace and our often well-intentioned eagerness to press for our own more limited vision.

Traditional resources tend to focus on matters of individual discernment (whether one should marry, for example, or what work one should do) or on matters closely connected to the internal life of a religious community. It requires some play to consider how guidance from the tradition may inform contemporary decision making about larger social or political questions. It is indeed possible. Ignatius of Loyola, the sixteenth-century spiritual guide and founder of the Jesuits, headquartered the fledgling order in the center of Rome, solidly in the intertwined political and ecclesiastical life of his day. From that urban center he founded schools, undertook charitable works, and sent missionaries throughout Europe and as far as India, Brazil, and Japan. What would it mean to practice the examination of consciousness that Ignatius taught with attentiveness to our own life "in the midst"? Instead of looking only at our personal sin, we could expand to ask how we knowingly or unknowingly participate in structural sin. How do we, every day, act for the greater glory of God in our work organization, in our church, in the way in which we vote, and in the policies we support? Where do we sit by silently and let injustice, ignorance, or inertia cause harm? How might we compose a rule for our own lives, to reflect our participation in God's redemptive work in the world?[3]

In recent times, the Jesuits have explicitly affirmed that the practice of discernment developed by their founder, Ignatius, can indeed ground action in the social, economic, political, and cultural spheres. The community has articulated its mission in terms of social justice—seeking structural change in the socioeconomic and political orders, working nonviolently for peace and reconciliation, mitigating the massive inequities produced by globalization, advancing the protection of human rights worldwide: "To discover and join the Lord, laboring to

Praying with Conviction and Humility

bring everything to its fullness, is central to the Jesuit way of proceeding. It is the Ignatian method of prayerful discernment, which can be described as a constant interplay between experience, reflection, decision, and action, in line with the Jesuit ideal of being 'contemplative in action.' "[4]

Asceticism: Spiritual Training

As farm workers marched to Sacramento on blistered feet, Chavez described the walk as a pilgrimage, a way of self-sacrifice and spiritual training. In his vision, they were walking both to bring attention to their struggle for economic justice and to recenter the movement. The pilgrimage was to be a kind of penitential Lenten discipline, turning the movement back to a commitment to nonviolence, strengthening it for the work ahead. Justice, he thought, would not come without sacrifice, discipline, self-examination. Faced again with disputes in the movement about the effectiveness of nonviolence, Chavez later went on a twenty-five-day fast to purify the movement. It was, again, a penitential act and a highly public stance on behalf of the cause. However imperfect these examples may be, and whatever questions they raise about the line between public relations technique and prayerful witness, they do carry traditional wisdom about a link between seeking justice and ascetic practice.

The Hebrew prophets insist that a true fast is imbedded in a just life: "Is this not the fast that I choose: to loose the bonds of injustice, to undo the thongs of the yoke, to let the oppressed go free, and to break every yoke?" (Isaiah 58:6). Fasting is not an end in and of itself; it is part of a way of life that seeks justice and transformation. Disciplines of self-restraint and penance are means of training us for the work of discipleship. The Christian tradition builds into the rhythm of liturgical life regular periods of prayer and fasting, linked to almsgiving. The willingness to deny oneself food, give up comfort and sustenance, and physically exert oneself affirms solidarity with those who are deprived of basic human necessities and dignity. Ascetic practice acknowledges too that we are sinful, that our desires may lead us astray; we need to train ourselves so as to live for a purpose beyond our immediate, individual will. It is no wonder that ascetic disciplines are a foundation of true prayer and a struggle for justice; they clear the way, in a sense, for us to be attentive to something beyond ourselves. They express a kind of humility that allows our prayer, our conviction, and our actions to be less tangled with self-interest, to be more discerning of God's purposes, to ring out more clearly and truly.

Eucharist: Lord, I Am Not Worthy

If any prayer practice is both humble and audacious, it must be the celebration of the Eucharist. For the community to affirm that God is really present in the ordinary stuff of bread and wine is just a stunning assertion. We have seen several communities express this bold conviction of faith as they gather for liturgy. To be offered the presence of Christ in the Eucharist is, at the same time, deeply humbling. Such is the prayer that one says during Mass right before receiving Communion: "Lord, I am not worthy to receive you, but only say the word and I shall be healed." In the acknowledgment of unworthiness, one opens to hear God's word; ultimately, it is God's word, not our own words, that brings healing.

As the farm workers and the prolife communities found, there is something about the celebration of the Eucharist that is deeply connected to a struggle for justice. Chavez broke his twenty-five-day fast by taking Communion. Farm worker supporters gathered for Mass said by priests wearing union logos on their stoles, consecrating wine made from union grapes. Prolife youths gathered for a Mass that sent them out into the streets of Washington, D.C., to march to the seat of American justice, the Supreme Court. Of course, the causes for which these communities gathered are not uncontroversial. Moreover, Christians are not at all agreed about the meaning of the Eucharist; some see it not as offering the real presence of Christ but rather as a remembrance of Jesus' last Passover meal. Sadly, longstanding divisions are evident, even within a practice that affirms and enacts Communion.

There is still inherent to the celebration of the Eucharist, imbedded in its logic and power, a deep call to justice and solidarity. As the bread is broken, so too the body is broken and in need of healing. Somehow, in the sharing of broken bread, the community re-members itself and recalls that we are meant to share the gifts of God's creation with all. The body cannot live without compassion and attention to all its parts. Amazingly, we are called to participate in God's creative and redemptive work in the world: "Through your goodness, we have this wine to offer, fruit of the vine and work of human hands." Participation in the Eucharist in turn sustains and sends forth the people of God to love and serve the Lord and one another.

Prayer as solidarity is actually a meeting place for many stories in this book. People in differing contexts prayed as a deep expression of solidarity with victims of injustice. They named those victims variously, yet what they shared was a deep need to acknowledge and affirm a connection with oppressed and suffering persons. Even when they were powerless to change the conditions of oppression, by praying in solidarity they could affirm shared humanity, along with spiritual sisterhood or brotherhood. "Never get tired of staying awake to pray for all the saints," counsels the letter to the Ephesians (6:18). To pray in solidarity is a way of re-membering the community and lifting up to God's power even those for whom we can do nothing else.

Lectio Divina

The apostle Paul exhorts the Thessalonians to "pray constantly." How do we live this out in the midst of a busy life of activity? One might object that ceaseless prayer is conceivable perhaps for cloistered monks and nuns who can devote their time most fully to prayer. Not so for the layperson necessarily involved in the work of caring for a family, holding down a job, and taking responsibility for those messy political structures important to the running of society. One may be tempted to abandon the biblical counsel. Still, its persistence in the tradition—from the desert elders to the nineteenth-century Russian pilgrim who uttered a short prayer with every breath—leads one to pause. Might there be a way to lean into the tradition of lectio divina as a way of incorporating constant prayer, even in an engaged life in the world? Built into the Benedictine way of life, resonating in the chanting of the contemporary Taizé community, the discipline of lectio divina can in fact meld with other ways of prayer that emerge from these stories. In a time of grief, one can pray the words of a lament psalm, slowly, one line, one question, over and over again ("Why do you sleep, O Lord?" Psalm 44:23). Seeking the courage to act prophetically, one could meditate on the words of the prophet Micah: "What does the Lord require of you but to do justice, and to love kindness, and to walk humbly with your God?" (6:8). The practice of chewing on the Word reminds us to slow down, listen deeply, and absorb the Scriptures into our everyday life. We might even hope to experience what the Russian pilgrim discovers in praying over and over again the Jesus Prayer: "Lord, Jesus Christ, have mercy on me, a sinner." Repeating these words time and time again, letting them move from his lips to his heart, the pilgrim discovers that prayer can flow as naturally as breath.

In several of the theology courses I have taught, I have asked the class to try "praying with the news." Each week students would cut out one newspaper article, pray with it during the week, and then out of that experience compose a prayer to share with the class. For some it was an experience of dissonance; how on earth does one pray about *this*? For others it opened up a way to engage concrete, complex situations in and through the lens of faith. One student composed a psalm out of her reading of the news. Another prayed a simple question, while one person wrote a litany. One student was an air force chaplain who went on to serve in Iraq. He has continued to pray with the news and encourage others to pray with him, grappling with the horrible realities of war, with the moral ambiguities of foreign policy. Praying with the news could be a new form of lectio divina, a way to prayerfully wrestle with the events happening all around us, integrating contemplation and action with the regularity of a daily newspaper.

Contemplative Prayer

The practice of lectio divina has long been understood as leading to contemplation of God. This is not irrelevant to an engaged spirituality. With the fervor and demands of the struggle for justice, there is still space for quiet. To quiet oneself is a humble and trusting posture integral to prayer, expressed so beautifully in the words of Psalm 131: "O Lord, my heart is not lifted up, my eyes are not raised too high; I do not occupy myself with things too great and too marvelous for me. But I have calmed and quieted my soul, like a weaned child with its mother" (1–2). In fact, our stories show that for many the more important their work, the more immersed they are in the real lives of human beings, the more important are regular moments of stillness. Tutu speaks of resting in the "divine serenity." Brother Roger spoke of drawing from the wellsprings of trust; only with that deep contemplative trust in God can we go out into the world as a "humble leaven of trust and peace within humanity." Contemplation can be the ground of action, a space for discernment, a reminder that our lives and work ultimately belong to God.

LORD, HAVE MERCY

When I stood outside the voting booth on Election Day and prayed a quick "Lord, have mercy," at the time it was as if to say, "I throw up my hands . . . make the best you can out of my very imperfect decision, and may it not bring more bad than good." I think now that there is a deeper way to understand that prayer.

In the gospel of Matthew, we read a story about two blind men who call out repeatedly to Jesus. Jesus and the disciples are leaving Jericho, followed by a large crowd, when the blind men sitting by the side of the road shout, "Lord, have mercy on us, Son of David!" While the crowd orders them to be quiet, they persist, shouting even more loudly, "Have mercy on us, Lord, Son of David!" Their shouted plea captures the mix of conviction and humility to which we are called in prayer. The men *shouted*—against those who would silence them—"Lord, have mercy," a phrase full of vulnerability and need. As they show, to pray humbly is not to be passive. Indeed, their persistence stops Jesus, who stands still and asks them: "What do you want me to do for you?" The two men ask for healing, for vision: "Lord, let our eyes be opened." Their prayer in fact is powerful—not in and of itself, but because it moves Jesus to compassion and draws forth Jesus' power. He touches their eyes. Immediately they regain their sight. Flowing from this exchange of humble prayer and Jesus' response is action, a new way of life: the two men follow Jesus (Matthew 20:29–34).

I wonder how this story might speak to those people gathered around my imaginary roundtable—Protestants and Catholics, prolife and prochoice, pro-Bush Republicans and antiwar activists, even South African widows and former security police. I imagine that it would be excruciatingly difficult for them to pray together. How would they find words with their disparate convictions, their varied sense of how God's grace may break into our world? How to find words in the face of the wounds they have inflicted on one another? How do they join hands when the body is broken? I wonder if perhaps they might find a simple phrase to pray, something like "Lord, have mercy." In this prayer, we are not absolved of human responsibility; we don't throw up our hands. We do acknowledge our need for God's graceful touch, for healing, for wholeness, for conversion. We recognize the reality of sin and the power of evil, and we acknowledge God's power to transform. In the din of our many words, it seems that we need this kind of simple prayer, which nonetheless carries within it a strong call to lead as just a life as we can, following Jesus, with eyes wide open, seeing, perceiving, attentive. We pray "Lord, have mercy" as we humbly ask God to take our best judgments, our moral intuitions, our deep convictions—to hold them and hear them and speak back to us, guiding us to a way of life that is in accordance with the purposes for which God has created us.

Notes

Chapter One

1. Joan Chittister OSB, *Wisdom Distilled from the Daily: Living the Rule of St. Benedict Today*. San Francisco: HarperSan-Francisco, 1990, pp. 29–30.
2. David Stevens, interviewed by author, Corrymeela, Ballycastle, Ireland, July 4, 2005.
3. Karl Barth, *Prayer*. Louisville: Westminster John Knox Press, 2002, p. 72.

Chapter Two

1. Macarius the Great, saying no. 19, in *The Sayings of the Desert Fathers: The Alphabetical Collection* (Benedicta Ward, trans.). London: Mowbray, 1975, p. 111.
2. John Cassian, *The Conferences*. New York: Newman Press, 1997, p. 386.
3. *Way of a Pilgrim*. New York: Doubleday, 1992, p. 33.
4. William Harmless S.J., *Desert Christians: An Introduction to the Literature of Early Monasticism*. Oxford: Oxford University Press, 2004.
5. Quotes are from Cassian (1997), p. 379.
6. Agathon, saying no. 9, in *Sayings of the Desert Fathers*, pp. 18–19.
7. Roberta Bondi, *To Pray and to Love: Conversations on Prayer with the Early Church*. Minneapolis: Fortress Press, 1991, pp. 14–15.

8. Douglas Burton-Christie, "Solitude, the Ground of Compassion." *Journal of Supervision and Training in Ministry,* 1997, *18,* 129–142.

9. Ignatius of Loyola, "The Autobiography." In George E. Ganss S.J. (ed.), *Ignatius of Loyola: Spiritual Exercises and Selected Works.* New York: Paulist Press, 1991, p. 68.

10. Ignatius of Loyola, "The Spiritual Exercises." In Ganss (1991), pp. 161, 163.

11. For passages related to the examen, see Ignatius of Loyola, "Spiritual Exercises," pp. 130–135.

12. Dennis Linn, Sheila Fabricant Linn, and Matthew Linn, *Sleeping with Bread: Holding What Gives You Life.* New York: Paulist Press, 1995.

13. Ignatius of Loyola, "Spiritual Exercises," p. 164.

14. Teresa of Avila, "The Book of Her Life." In *The Collected Works of St. Teresa of Avila, Vol. 1* (Kieran Kavanaugh and Otilio Rodriguez, trans.). Washington, D.C.: ICS, 1987, p. 96.

15. Teresa of Avila, "Book of Her Life," p. 88.

16. Teresa of Avila, "Book of Her Life," p. 87.

17. Teresa of Avila, "Book of Her Life," p. 96.

18. Teresa of Avila, "Book of Her Life," p. 257.

19. Teresa of Avila, "Book of Her Life," p. 159.

20. Teresa of Avila, "Book of Her Life," p. 181.

21. Teresa of Avila, "Book of Her Life," pp. 178, 118.

22. Cassian (1997), p. 330.

23. For a helpful book that gives a new look at the relationship between the mystical tradition and social change in historical contexts, see Janet K. Ruffing (ed.), *Mysticism and Social Transformation.* Syracuse, N.Y.: Syracuse University Press, 2001.

Chapter Three

1. In a 2005 survey of 270 church members, more than half held a graduate degree and 42 percent enjoyed a household

income of more than $100,000. Roughly four out of five were white and 12 percent were Hispanic. Members also were quite stable, with 65 percent living in the area for twenty years or more and about 75 percent saying they did not expect to move from South Florida in the next few years. "Results of Member Survey: Coral Gables Congregational Church," July 25, 2005.

2. Phrases in quotes in this paragraph are all drawn directly from the "Independent Review Panel (IRP) Final Draft Report on the Free Trade Area of the Americas (FTAA) Inquiry, June 2004." http://www.miamidade.gov/irp/Library/final_draft_06-11-04.pdf.

3. Rev. Donna Schaper and Roy D. Wasson detail these and other occurrences in their paper, "Report on Governmental Interference with Activities of Coral Gables Congregational Church During Free Trade of Americas Summit Conference October-November, 2003, Miami-Dade County, Florida," paper presented at Samford University Conference on Christianity and Human Rights, Fourth Annual Lilly Fellows Program, National Research Conference, Birmingham, Alabama, Nov. 11–14, 2004. For full text of paper, see http://www.samford.edu/lillyhumanrights/papers/Schaper_Report.pdf.

4. Schaper and Wasson (2003).

5. See People for the American Way, www.pfaw.org.

6. See Coalition of Immokalee, www.ciw-online.org.

7. See the United Church of Christ, www.ucc.org/justice/boycotts.

8. www.ucc.org/justice/action/w030402.htm.

9. See National Council of Churches, www.nccusa.org. For a list of endorsing organizations, see the National Farm Worker Ministry, www.nfwm.org.

10. See "Across the UCC: UCC Churches Find Positive Ways to Work for Peace," *United Church News,* Dec. 2002. http://www.ucc.org/ucnews/dec02/across.htm.

11. See "Statement of United Church of Christ Leaders Opposing U.S. War Against Iraq," Sept. 13, 2002. http://www.ucc.org/justice/iraq.htm. Signers of the letter included the UCC Collegium of Officers, numerous conference ministers, and several seminary presidents.

12. Noel Cleland, e-mail message to author, Jan. 18, 2006.

13. This quote from a church member is found in the minutes of the CGCC Congregation annual meeting held on Sunday, Jan. 28, 2001.

14. Schaper, interviewed by author, Mar. 11, 2003.

15. Comments by Schaper to the Coral Gables Congregational Church council, Feb. 19, 2003.

16. Mary Eaton, interviewed by author, Jan. 6, 2006.

17. John Risley, "Liberation Spirituality." *Spirituality Today,* Summer 1983, *35*(2), 117–126.

18. Jon Sobrino, "Monseñor Romero, a Salvadoran and a Christian." *Spiritus: A Journal of Christian Spirituality,* 2001, *1*(2), 143–155.

19. Sobrino, *Spirituality of Liberation: Toward Political Holiness.* Maryknoll, N.Y.: Orbis Books, 1988, p. 67.

20. Sobrino, "Christian Prayer and New Testament Theology: A Basis for Social Justice and Spirituality." In M. Fox (ed.), *Western Spirituality: Historical Roots, Ecumenical Routes.* Santa Fe, N.M.: Bear, 1981, pp. 91–92.

21. Sacred Congregation for the Doctrine of the Faith, *Instruction on Certain Aspects of "Theology of Liberation."* Washington, D.C.: U.S. Catholic Conference, 1984.

22. Jon Arthur, interviewed by Kirk VanGilder, research assistant to author, Jan. 30, 2006.

23. Beverly Ross, pastoral prayer, Coral Gables Congregational Church, Nov. 7, 2004.

24. Ross, interviewed by author, Jan. 8, 2005.

25. Eaton, interviewed by author, Jan. 6, 2006.

26. Anonymous upon request, interviewed by Nicole Johnson, research assistant to author, Feb. 6, 2006.

27. Christine Elliott, interviewed by Johnson, research assistant to author, July 12, 2005.

28. Anonymous upon request, interviewed by Johnson, research assistant to author, July 12, 2005.

29. Rev. Schaper's comment was quoted in the article "What Does It Mean to Be a 'United' Church?" *United Church News,* Oct. 2003. http://www.ucc.org/ucnews/oct03/soapbox.htm.

30. Donna Schaper, "What Does It Mean to Be a 'United' Church?" *United Church News,* Oct. 2003. http://www.ucc.org/ucnews/oct03/soapbox.htm.

31. "Seeking a Senior Minister," published on the church Website, http://www.coralgablescongregational.net/Administrator/Documents/PSC_1-Page_Summary2.pdf.

Chapter Four

1. World Council of Churches, "Harare Declaration." 1985; reprint, World Council of Churches Programme to Combat Racism. PCR Information: Reports and Background Papers. Southern Africa: The Harare and Ai-Gams Declarations: A Call for Freedom and Independence for South Africa and Namibia, no. 23, 1986, p. 16. Citations are to the World Council of Churches Programme edition.

2. Quotes in this paragraph are by the photographer, Sam Nzima, and Antoinette Sithole, respectively. Lucille Davie, "The Day Hector Pieterson Died." June 15, 2005. http://www.safrica.info/ess_info/sa_glance/history/hector-pieterson.htm.

3. Charles Villa-Vicencio, "Introduction." In Allan Boesak and C. Villa-Vicencio (eds.), *A Call for an End to Unjust Rule.* Edinburgh: Saint Andrew Press, 1986, p. 16.

4. "A Theological Rationale and a Call to Prayer for an End to Unjust Rule." In Boesak and Villa-Vicencio (1986), p. 26.

5. John de Gruchy, "Introduction." In J. de Gruchy (ed.), *Cry Justice! Prayers, Meditations, and Readings from South Africa.* Maryknoll, N.Y.: Orbis Books, 1986, p. 36.

6. Villa-Vicencio, "Some Refused to Pray: The Moral Impasse of the English-Speaking Churches." In Boesak and Villa-Vicencio (1986), p. 44.

7. Villa-Vicencio, "Some Refused to Pray," p. 33.

8. Villa-Vicencio, "Some Refused to Pray," p. 45.

9. "Statement by Prof. Ben Engelbrecht and Some Staff Members of the Department of Religious Studies, University of Witwatersrand." In Boesak and Villa-Vicencio (1986), pp. 165–167.

10. Philip Russell, "Pastoral Letter of 7 June 1985." In Boesak and Villa-Vicencio (1986), pp. 172–175.

11. Peter Storey, "Prayer in the Anti-Apartheid Struggle." Unpublished paper, Prayer and Social Engagement Conference hosted by Church and Theology in the Contemporary World Project, Berlin, May 27–29, 2004, p. 5. Storey here quotes directly from his President's Update, which was sent to all Methodist leaders on June 14, 1985.

12. "Statement by Prof. Ben Engelbrecht."

13. World Council of Churches, *The Kairos Document: Challenge to the Church: A Theological Comment on the Political Crisis in South Africa.* Geneva: World Council of Churches, 1985, pp. 16, 22, 23, 29.

14. Boesak, "What Belongs to Caesar? Once Again Romans 13." In Boesak and Villa-Vicencio (1986), p. 139.

15. For helpful commentary on this text, see Joseph A. Fitzmyer, SJ, *Romans: A New Translation with Introduction and Commentary.* (Anchor Bible.) New York: Doubleday, 1993, pp. 661–676.

16. See Neil Elliott, *Liberating Paul: The Justice of God and the Politics of the Apostle.* Maryknoll, N.Y.: Orbis Books, 1994. I also am indebted to my colleague James Walters for his comments on the subject in the seminar Church and Theology in the Contemporary World, Boston University, Jan. 25, 2006.

17. Boesak, "What Belongs to Caesar?"

18. Karl Barth, "Church and State." In *Community, State, and Church: Three Essays.* Garden City, N.Y.: Anchor Books, 1960.

Chapter Five

1. California Newsreel, "Long Night's Journey into Day." http://www.newsreel.org/transcripts/longnight.htm. The Website content is a transcript of *Long Night's Journey into Day* (VHS, DVD), producer and director Frances Reid, director Deborah Hoffmann (San Francisco: California Newsreel, 2000).
2. Storey, "Prayer in the Anti-Apartheid Struggle," p. 3.
3. Terry Swicegood, "Funeral at Craddock." *Christianity and Crisis,* Sept. 16, 1985, p. 343. Additional details about the funeral come from "Mammoth Funeral Held in South Africa for Assassinated Anti-Apartheid Leaders." Xinhua General Overseas News Service, July 22, 1985.
4. See http://www.anc.org.za/misc/nkosi.html#english2 for the current English version of "Nkosi Sikelela iAfrika."
5. J. David Pleins, *The Psalms: Songs of Tragedy, Hope, and Justice.* Maryknoll, N.Y.: Orbis Books, 1993, p. 32.
6. Reuters, "Tutu Defies South African Court Order with Criticism of Apartheid at Funeral." *Toronto Star,* Dec. 20, 1988, p. A14.
7. William E. Smith, "Black Rage, White Fist." *Time,* Aug. 5, 1985, p. 26.
8. Piet Meiring, "The Baruti Versus the Lawyers: The Role of Religion in the TRC Process." In C. Villa-Vicencio and W. Verwoerd (eds.), *Looking Back, Reaching Forward: Reflections on the Truth and Reconciliation Commission of South Africa.* Cape Town: University of Cape Town Press, 2000a, pp. 123–131.
9. Meiring (2000a), p. 124.
10. Desmond Tutu, "Gifts of Justice, Mercy, and Compassion." In *South Africa's Human Spirit: An Oral Memoir of the Truth*

and Reconciliation Commission, Vol. 1: "Bones of Memory," audio recordings of the Human Rights Violation (HRV) hearing, East London, South Africa, Apr. 15, 1996. South Africa: SABC News Production, 2000.

11. South Africa Truth and Reconciliation Commission. *Human Rights Violations: Submissions—Questions and Answers.* "Nomonde Calata." Apr. 16, 1996. http://www.doj.gov.za/trc; go to Human Rights Violation (HRV) Committee transcripts, East London, Nomonde Calata.

12. Tutu, *No Future Without Forgiveness.* New York: Doubleday, 1999, p. 148.

13. Meiring (2000a), p. 126.

14. P. Meiring, "The God of Surprises." *REC Mission Bulletin,* Apr. 2000b, *20*(1). http://rec.gospelcom.net/MB-April00meiring.html.

15. California Newsreel, "Long Night's Journey into Day."

16. Meiring (2000b).

17. California Newsreel, "Long Night's Journey into Day."

18. California Newsreel, "Long Night's Journey into Day."

19. Meiring (2000b).

20. Amnesty was refused in a decision of 1999. South Africa Truth and Reconciliation Commission, Amnesty Committee, "Application in Terms of Section 18 of the Promotion of National Unity and Reconciliation Act, No. 34 of 1995." http://www.doj.gov.za/trc/decisions/1999/ac990350.htm.

21. California Newsreel, "Long Night's Journey into Day."

22. Tutu (1999), p. 201.

23. Tutu (1999), p. 201.

24. Tutu (1999), p. 31.

25. Tutu (1999), p. 82.

Chapter Six

1. For a traditional account of the appearance, see, for example, http://www.sancta.org/juandiego.html.

2. Andres G. Guerrero, *A Chicano Theology*. Maryknoll, N.Y.: Orbis Books, 1987, pp. 105–106.

3. Richard Griswold del Castillo, *The Birth of La Causa*. Excerpt quoted in Richard W. Etulain (ed.), *César Chávez: A Brief Biography with Documents*. Boston: Bedford/St. Martin's, 2002, p. 86.

4. Spencer Bennett, "Civil Religion in a New Context: The Mexican-American Faith of César Chávez." In Gustavo Benavides and M. W. Daly (eds.), *Religion and Political Power*. Albany: State University of New York Press, 1989, p. 159.

5. Susan Ferriss and Ricardo Sandoval, *The Fight in the Fields: Cesar Chavez and the Farmworkers Movement*. New York: Harvest/HBJ Books, 1997, p. 119.

6. Griswold Del Castillo (2002), p. 90.

7. Ferriss and Sandoval (1997), p. 117.

8. See text of "El Plan de Delano," available, for example, at http://www.aztlan.net/plandela.htm.

9. Bennett (1989), p. 161.

10. Jacques Levy, *Cesar Chavez: Autobiography of La Causa*. New York: Norton, 1975, p. 272.

11. Telephone conversation among Fred Ross, Dolores Huerta, and Saul Alinsky during Chavez's fast, cited in Etulain (2002), p. 43.

12. Ferriss and Sandoval (1997), p. 143.

13. Levy (1975), pp. 277, 276.

14. Etulain (2002), p. 36.

15. Ferriss and Sandoval (1997), p. 143.

16. Richard J. Foster, *Celebration of Discipline: The Path to Spiritual Growth*. San Francisco: HarperSanFrancisco, 1998, pp. 48–49.

Chapter Seven

1. Rev. Tom Davis relates this story, including the words in quotations, in his book *Sacred Work: Planned Parenthood*

and *Its Clergy Alliances.* New Brunswick, N.J.: Rutgers University Press, 2005, pp. 1–2.

2. Davis (2005), pp. 2, 6.

3. See testimony of Mary Therese Weyrich, "Why I Go There." Priests for Life. http://www.priestsforlife.org/testimony/marywtest.htm.

4. Steve Angrisano, "We Have Come" (OCP Publications, 2005).

5. Rev. Gerard Francik, homily, Youth Mass, Jan. 23, 2006, Washington, D.C.

6. All quotes are found in "From Generation to Generation: Celebrating 30 Years of Faithful Reproductive Choices" (program), An Interfaith Convocation, New York Avenue Presbyterian Church, Washington, D.C., Jan. 22, 2003.

7. Rev. Ignacio Castuera, interviewed by Nicole Johnson, research assistant to author, Dec. 13, 2005.

8. Castuera interview.

9. See Helpers of God's Precious Infants, "About Us" and "Who Are the Helpers of God's Precious Infants." http://members.aol.com/infants1.

10. Steve Kloehn, "Abortion Clinic Vigil to Bring Cardinal Out." *Chicago Tribune,* June 25, 1999.

11. Helpers of God's Precious Infants. http://members.aol.com/infants1.

12. Helpers of God's Precious Infants, http://members.aol.com/infants1; Priests for Life, http://www.priestsforlife.org.

13. See Crossroads Website, http://www.crossroadswalk.org/About/.

14. All quotes from walkers found on Crossroads Website, http://www.crossroadswalk.org/walkers/walk_profiles.asp.

15. Prayer written by the Reverend G. Anthony Hoeltzel and read at the memorial service for Shannon Lowney and Leanne Nichols, held on Jan. 22, 1995, at the Cathedral of St. John the Divine. Reprinted in Davis (2005), pp. 203–204.

16. All quotes come from material from Priests for Life, http://www.priestsforlife.org.

17. See Priests for Life, "Prayer Resources" and "Meditations for Pro-Life Stations of the Cross." http://www.priestsforlife.org.

18. See Religious Coalition for Reproductive Choice, "Sermons and Prayers." www.rcrc.org/resources/sermons_prayers/providers_prayers.htm.

19. Priests for Life Website, link for "Prayer Resources." www.priestsforlife.org/prayers/index.htm.

20. Rev. Kathleen Buckley, "Ash Wednesday Reflections—To Repent of Our Silence." *Conscience: A Publication Dedicated to Reproductive Freedom for Women* (Adirondack Religious Coalition for Choice), Apr. 1998, 9(3), 3–4.

Chapter Eight

1. Kathryn Spink, *A Universal Heart: The Life and Vision of Brother Roger of Taizé.* San Francisco: HarperSanFrancisco, 1986, p. 28.

2. Peter C. Moore, *Tomorrow Is Too Late: Taizé, An Experiment in Christian Community.* London: Mowbray, 1970.

3. See Taizé, http://www.Taizé.com.

4. Quotes and information in this paragraph are taken from *A Hope to Be Shared: Young Russians in Taizé.* Taizé, France: Les Presses de Taizé, 1999, pp. 5–6. The Taizé Website also mentions the visits of brothers to Eastern Europe beginning in 1962.

5. Brother Roger, Preface to *Prayer for Each Day.* Chicago: GIA, 1997, p. v.

6. "How Can We Keep on Praying Together?" In *Chants de Taizé,* 2003–04 songbook.

7. Brother Roger, Preface, p. v.

8. Paraphrased from Guigo II, "The Ladder of Monks: A Letter on the Contemplative Life." In Guigo II, *The Ladder of Monks: A Letter on the Contemplative Life and Twelve Meditations*

(Edmund Colledge and James Walsh, trans.). Kalamazoo, Mich.: Cistercian, 1979.

9. William Johnston (ed.), *The Cloud of Unknowing and the Book of Privy Counseling.* New York: Doubleday, 1973, pp. 49, 55.

10. Teresa of Avila, *Book of Her Life,* pp. 113, 164.

11. Johnston (1973), p. 53.

12. Taizé Community, *Taizé: Songs for Prayer.* Chicago: GIA, 1998, p. v.

13. Brother Roger, "Letter from Taizé: To the Wellsprings of Joy," presented at Pilgrimage of Trust young adult meeting, Hamburg, Germany, Dec. 29, 2003–Jan. 2, 2004. This letter was also a starting point for reflection at weekly meetings in Taizé throughout 2004.

14. http://www.Taizé.com.

15. http://www.Taizé.com.

Chapter Nine

1. Karl Rahner, "Prayer." In *The Practice of Faith: A Handbook of Contemporary Spirituality.* New York: Crossroad, 1992, p. 85.

2. Agathon, saying no. 15, in *Sayings of the Desert Fathers,* p. 19.

3. Note that the Woodstock Theological Center in Washington, D.C., which was founded by Jesuits in 1974, has attempted to bring just such reflection into various initiatives. For example, the program on Social Ethics in Business invites business leaders to integrate their faith and work through the perspective Ignatius offers in the "Principle and Foundation," what then-program director J. Michael Stebbins called the "human family's 'mission statement.'" Program participants ask, What is business for? Then, drawing on the Ignatian examen as an aid to discernment, they come to make decisions that better serve those ultimate aims; they

gradually gain the freedom to choose well and carry out their decisions. See Woodstock Theological Center, http://www.georgetown.edu/centers/woodstock/report/r-fea56.htm.

4. "Documents of the Thirty-Fourth General Congregation of the Society of Jesus" (document 26, no. 8). Saint Louis: Institute of Jesuit Sources, 1995, p. 237. On justice concerns of the Jesuits, see, for example, document 3, "Our Mission and Justice."

The Author

————

Claire Wolfteich is associate professor of practical theology and spiritual formation at Boston University. Her publications include *Navigating New Terrain: Work and Women's Spiritual Lives* and *American Catholics Through the Twentieth Century: Spirituality, Lay Experience, and Public Life*. She codirects the Center for Practical Theology at Boston University and works with urban pastors throughout the country through the center's Sustaining Urban Pastoral Excellence Project, to which she brings experience in leading ecumenical small group formation and spiritual renewal. She directs the Pastoral and Spiritual Formation program and the Spiritual Formation and Church Life Project at the university. She has also served as advisor to the National Conference of Catholic Bishops on issues of women and lay spirituality. She holds a Ph.D. from the University of Chicago and received her B.A. from Yale University.

Index

A

Abortion, 1, 10, 12, 121–143, 167–168

Abortion clinics, xvii, 132–135, 136, 137–138. *See also* Planned Parenthood clinics

Abortion providers, 128, 133, 138, 139, 140

Action: attention diverted from, 47, 154, 155; blending contemplation and, 147, 154, 155, 156–157, 161, 179–180; contemplative in, 174; discernment grounding, 173–174; finding the correct relationship between prayer and, 47; prayer in, synthesis in, 45; tension between contemplation and, 155. *See also* Politics; Social action

Acts: 1:14, 4; 2:42, 4; 2:46-47, 4

African American congregations, 45

African National Congress flag, 80

African worldview, 97

African Xhosa language, 82

Afrikaans, 59

Agathon, 19–20, 165

Agendas, personal, using prayer as a tool to advance, problem of, xv

Alinsky, S., 112

Almsgiving, 175

Alois, 160

"Amazing Grace" hymn, 122

Ambiguity: of foreign policy, 179; power and, 28–31

American nuns and lay missionary, murder of, 46

Amnesty: applying for, 91, 93; granting of, 88; refusing application for, 94, 190*n*20

Anglican archbishops, 66, 80, 87

Anglican churches, 66, 87

Antiwar billboards, 42–43

Apartheid, defined, 58

Apartheid in South Africa: boycott during, 42; ending, call to pray for, 57–76; entering into the story of, 12; injustices of, praying through, 77–98; path of prayer that arose during, 170–171; and questioning contemplation, 154; repeal of, 87; student response to the bold prayer of, xvi–xvii

Ascesis, meaning of, 106

Ascetic practice, 106, 109, 174–175

Ash Wednesday, 114

Atheism, 92

Atheists, 111

Augustine, 109

Authentic prayer. *See* True prayer

Authentic spirituality, 164

Authoritarianism, 53–54

Authority, highest, 74

Aztec civilization, 102

B

Babylonian captors, cry for vengeance against, 85

Babylonian sack of Jerusalem, 68

Bahia, Brazil, quiet witness in, 148

Balance, importance of, 7
Baptism, 96, 102
Baptist churches: members drawn from, 34; worship emphasis in, 50
Baptist prolife supporters, 127
Barefoot walking, 109
Barmen Declaration, 74
Barrett, J., 129
Barth, K., 11, 64, 74–75, 166
Benedict, St., 7
Benedictine tradition, 7, 178
Benedict's Rule, 7, 150
Bethlehem, pilgrimage to, 108
Bible reading: interpretation during, and discernment, 15; in monastic communities, 7; in the Taizé community, 150–151, 156, 178. *See also specific books of the Bible*
Billboards, antiwar, 42–43
Body, the: brokenness in, 141–143, 176, 181; identity of, prayer expressing the, 168–169
Boesak, A., 60–61, 73, 74, 81
Boff, L., 45
Bondi, R., 21
Boston Roman Catholic archdiocese, 50
Botha, P. W., 61
Boycotts, 39–42, 86, 101, 102, 111, 112. *See also* Strikes
Brazil, quiet witness in, 148
Brazilian theologian, 45
Brigid, St., 110
Brookline Planned Parenthood clinic, 137
Brown, P., 111
Buckley, K., 141–142
Buddhist prochoice supporters, 128
Burton-Christie, D., 21
Bush, G. W., 1, 38, 54, 128
Business leaders, invitation to, 194n3

C

Calata, F., 77–78, 80, 90, 92
Calata, N., 80, 90, 91–92, 93, 94, 95, 97
Calata, T., 91
California farm worker's movement, story of, 12, 99–119. *See also* Farm workers
Candlelight prayer vigil, 40
Canterbury Tales, The (Chaucer), 108
Cape Town, South Africa, 66, 67
Capitol Hill, 127, 128
Carmelite monastery, 26
Carmelite order, reformation of the, 28
Cassian, J., 18, 19, 29
Castuera, I., 130–132
Cathedral of St. John the Devine, 137, 139
Catherine of Siena, 30
Catholic churches: and the farm worker movement, 116; members drawn from, 34
Catholic hierarchy, 48
Catholic practices and traditions. *See specific practices and traditions*
Catholic prolife supporters: schoolchildren as, 122, 126; in shared prayer with Protestant prochoice supporters, experience of, 141–142; young adult, pilgrimage by, 135–137
Catholics and Protestants: conflict between, seeking reconciliation for, 7–8; contemplative community composed of, 146, 148; in shared prayer, but with different convictions on abortion, 141–142
Caution, voices of, 65–67, 76
Ceaseless prayer, 4, 18, 19, 177–178
Charitable acts, 30

Chatfield, L., 118

Chaucer, G., 108

Chavez, C.: background on, 100–102; conviction of, 167; entering into the story of, 12; fasting by, 112–113, 114, 115–116, 117–119, 174, 176; march by, 104–107, 110–111; student response to, xvii; symbol for, 103

Chavez, H., 101, 112

Chittister, J., 7

Choice, the term, refusal to cede, to the prochoice movement, 126–127

Choices: focusing our, 24; as often messy, 10; prolife stance on, 127

Christ. *See* Jesus

Christian community: behind the Iron Curtain, visiting, 149; division in the unity of, 141–143, 148; in Northern Ireland, 7–8. *See also specific communities*

Christian pilgrimage, history of, 108–109. *See also* Pilgrimage

Christian prochoice supporters, 128

Christian tradition, 13–14. *See also specific traditions*

Christian way of life: prayer and the, 17–31, 59, 65; as restless, 108–109

Christianity, responsibility to protect, believing in, 92

Christians, conservative and liberal, 1, 2, 34, 48

Christmas, 158

Church abuse, response to, questioning, xiii

"Church and State" (Barth), 75

Church attendance, 49

Church member survey, results of, for Coral Gables, 184–185n1

Church of the Province of South Africa, 66

Church of the Reconciliation, 145, 146, 149–150, 155–156, 160

Church Partnership program of Planned Parenthood, 130

Church social action groups, 3

Churches. *See specific church*

Civil Rights Act of 1964, 100

Civil rights movement, 35, 100, 104–105, 124

Clarity, points of, 25

Claudius, 73

Cleland, N., 42, 43

Clergy Advisory Board of Planned Parenthood

"Clergy Voices" journal, 130

Cloud of Unknowing, The (Anonymous), 153, 155

Coalition of Immokalee Workers (CIW), 39–40

Coffin, W. S., 35

Collective bargaining law, call to establish a, 111

Communal prayer: collective nature of, 50; by the desert elders, 19; gathering for, 29; and a place for discernment, 71–72, 75–76; in the Taizé community, 149–150, 151

Communion, 127, 147, 151, 152, 175, 176

Communism, 92

Communist flag, 80

Community: of the church, prayer rooted in the life and teachings of, 27, 29; of prayer, life as a, 5; re-membering the, way of, 176, 177

Complexity, 11, 86

Conferences (Cassian), 18

Confessing Church movement, 74

Confession, going to, 110

Confessions (Augustine), 109

Confusion: about spirituality, 30; prayer amidst, 8–11

Congregational tensions, over politics, xiv, 12, 33–34, 35, 36–45, 48–55

Consciousness, daily examination of, 24–25

Conservative Christians, 1, 2, 34, 48

Consolation, 23

Constant prayer, 4, 18, 19, 177–178

Constantine I, 108

Contemplation: in action, 174; blending action and, 147, 154, 155, 156–157, 161, 179–180; as Christian practice, 152–154; distinguishing, from meditation, 153; requiring silence, 156; road to, 150; silent, 151; tension between action and, 155

Contemplative community, example of a. *See* Taizé community

Contemplative life, exclusive focus on, issue with, 47

Contemplative model, 153–154

Contemplative prayer: as a gift from God, 153; path of, 179–180; power of, 161; questioning, xvii, 147, 154, 161

Contemporary Western culture, 5–6

Controversial and divisive issue, one of the most. *See* Abortion

Conversation, stimulating, 15–16

Conviction and humility, praying with, 163–181

Convictions, being able to pray our, importance of, 143

Coral Gables Congregational Church (CGCC), 33–34, 35, 36–45, 48–55, 184–185n1

Corinthian community, 96

1 Corinthians: 1:10, 96; 12:12-13, 96; 12:26, 97; 12:27, 96

Corrymeela Community, Northern Ireland, 7–8

Counterculture, 5–6

Cradock Four, the: expressing remorse for role in murders of, 93; funeral for, 79, 80, 81–82, 85, 86, 97; lament prayer for, 171; misguided belief about, 92–93; story of, 77–78; widows of, 78, 79, 80, 90, 93–94

Crossroads organization, 136

Cuban Americans, 34

Culture: contemporary westernized, 5–6; Mexican, 113

D

Daily examen, 24–25

Dakar, Senegal, quiet witness in, 148

Davis, B., 124

Davis, T., 123–124, 131

de Gruchy, J., 63–64

Defiant prayer. *See* Raised fists, praying with

Delano, California, 99, 100, 101, 102, 105, 106, 110

Desert elders, 14, 17–20, 22, 28, 29, 165

Desolation, 23

Detachment, meaning of, misunderstanding the, 30

Deuteronomy, 127; 18:20-22, 72; 30:19, 129

Devil, the (Satan), 19, 27

Diego, J., 102, 103, 127

Discernment: aid to, 25; as a critical part of prayer, 26–27, 172; Ignatian teaching on, 14; and interpretation of the Bible, 15; place for, 71–72, 75–76, 165, 179–180; problem of, 10; process of, 23, 24, 25, 172–174; seeking to grow in, 17; witness to the importance of, 29

Disciples, the: awaiting the return of Jesus, 4; Jesus teaching, 9, 78, 85–86, 98, 118; and the Last Supper, 154; leaving Jericho, 180

Divine Office, saying the, 7, 19

Divine serenity, sharing in, 95–97, 179

Divisive and controversial issue, one of the most. *See* Abortion

Donegal, Ireland, 109

Dorotheos of Gaza, 20–21

Dr. Seuss character, 126

Dutch Reformed Church, 60, 63–64, 93, 94

E

East London, South Africa, 79

Easter, 105, 111

Eastern Orthodox spirituality, 18

Eaton, M., 44–45, 49–50

"El Plan de Delano" (Valdez), 106–107

El Salvador, 45–46

Election Day, 1–2, 180

Election year, prayer in an, 1–16

Eli, 71

Enemies: loving one's, 79; threats from, lamenting, 83

Engagement, prayerful, with the world, 164

Environment, hurting the, 54

Ephesians: 4:1-5, 142; 6:11-17, 134–135; 6:18, 97, 135, 177; 6:18-19, 5

Episcopalian priest, 139

Equal opportunity mandate, 100

Eschatological symbol, 65

Ethical Humanists, 128

Ethinic/racial issues. *See Racial entries*

Eucharist, the: celebration of, 12, 95, 175–177; desert elders gathering for, 19; fasting and, 114–117, 119; literal meaning of, 115

Eucharistic Prayer, the, 115, 176–177

Evangelical prolife supporters, 127

Evil, confrontation with, fight against abortion seen as, 134–135

Examination of consciousness, 24–25

Ezekiel 13:6, 72

F

Faith: critical practice of, 72; embodied in the concrete praxis of liberation, 45; engaging our, with the world around us, issues surrounding, xiii; living into the, complexity of, 86; separation of, from politics, 69; shared, prayer at the heart of, 3–5; social action springing from and reflecting, 5, 167; that seeks understanding, prayer as part of, 29. *See also* Spirituality

False prayer, 167

False prophets, 68, 72, 172

False spirituality, 46, 69

False worship, 68

Farm workers, xvii, 12, 39–42, 99–119, 167, 174, 176

Fasting: by Cesar Chavez, 12, 112–113, 114, 115–116, 117–119, 174, 176; and the Eucharist, 114–117; hunger strike vs., 118; by Irish pilgrims, 109, 110; by Jesus, 105; true, 174–175. *See also* Pilgrimage

Fatima, pilgrimage to, 108

Female minister, breaking ground as a, 35

Feminist movement, 100

Fetus, prolife view of the, 133
Fight in the Field, The (Ferriss and
    Sandoval), 117
Filipino immigrant farm work-
    ers, 100, 102. *See also* Farm
    workers
Fists raised, image of. *See* Raised
    fists, praying with
Florida: attack at abortion clinic
    in, 138; car crash tragedy in,
    8–9; church congregation
    in, story of tensions in, 33–55
Foley, M., 137
Foreign policy, 1, 10, 179
Forgiveness: call for, 78, 85–86,
    160; connecting prayer and,
    79; in South Africa, 12, 78,
    87, 89, 93, 94
Foster, R., 118
France, liberation of, 148. *See also*
    Taizé community
Francik, G., 126–127
Francis of Assisi, St., 30, 101
Free market, the, 53
Free Speech Award, 39
Free Trade Agreement of the
    Americas (FTAA), 36–39
Friendship, prayer as, 25–28
Fundamentalism, 53
Funerals, 79, 80, 81–82, 85, 86, 87,
    97, 160

G

Gandhi, M., 101, 112
Gay and lesbian marriage/unions,
    1, 34, 50–51
General Conference of the United
    Methodist Church, 41
Generous living, example of,
    21–25
Germany, unjust rule in, 74, 148
"Go Make a Difference" hymn,
    127
Golden Gate Bridge, California,
    135

Goniwe, M., 77–78, 80, 93, 94
Government: boycotts against the,
    86; obedience to, questioning,
    73–75; praying for the, 58, 59,
    62, 66, 75; taking out the,
    prayer calling for, 57–58,
    60–63, 64, 66, 67, 70, 73, 76.
    See also Politics
Graduate degrees, church mem-
    bers holding, in Coral
    Gables, 184n1
Grape boycott, 101, 102, 105, 112
Greenwich Village church, New
    York City, 54
Guides, benefiting from, 15–16
Guigo II, 150
Gunn, D., 128, 138
Gutiérrez, G., 47

H

Hajj, 107
Hannah, 70–71
Hell's Kitchen neighborhood,
    quiet witness in, 148
Helpers of God's Precious Infants,
    134
Heresy: apartheid declared as, 58,
    61; prochoice prayer seen as,
    139; ruthless rooting out of,
    period of, 157
Herrera, A. H., 105–106
Hewbrew prayer book, 83. *See also*
    Psalms, the
Hill, P., 138
Hitler, A., 74
Hoeltzel, G. A., 138–139
Homosexual marriage/unions, 1,
    34, 50–51
Hope: in God, 85; living in, 65;
    opening with, time of, 105;
    prayer ending with, 84;
    reminder of, for social
    activists, 8
Horton the Elephant, 126
Hospitality, 20, 157, 158

Household income, of church members in Coral Gables, 184*n*1

Huerta, D., 101, 103–104, 111, 113

Human knowledge, limitations of, process prone to, 10

Humanity, shared, 97

Humility: praying with conviction and, 163–181; true, 27; and trust, as integral, 18; witness to the importance of, 29

Hunger strike vs. fasting, 118

Hypocritical prayer, 68

I

Idealism, 8

Identity, prayer as expression of, 168–169

Ignatian spirituality, 14, 24, 25, 173–174, 194–195*n*3

Ignatius of Loyola, 21–25, 28, 29, 173, 194*n*3

Illegal abortions, 123, 124, 128

Immokalee workers, 39–40, 41

Income, household, of church members in Coral Gables, 184*n*1

Independent Review Panel (IRC), 37

Indian independence, struggle for, 112

Individual discernment, focus on, 172–173

Injustice: of apartheid, lament over, 82–87, 170–171; praying through, 77–98

Inquisition, the, 27, 157

Intercessory prayer, 4, 50–51, 75, 95–96, 97

Interfaith Christian prochoice supporters, 128

Interfaith marriage, 35

Intimacy with God, 21

Iona, pilgrimage to, 108

Iraq war, the, xiii, 1, 42–43, 179

Ireland: Christian community in, 7–8; pilgrimage in, 109–110

Iron Curtain, the, visiting Christians behind, 149

Isaac, 18, 19, 29

Isaiah: 10:1-2, 41; 58:3-7, 117; 58:6, 174

Islam, 107

Israel: and the false prophets, 72; history of, horrible time during the, 68; lament involving the people of, 83, 85, 171; prophetic movement of, 131. *See also* Jerusalem

Israel, M., 129

J

Jeremiah, 68, 122; 14:11-12, 68; 21:12, 68; 22:13, 68; 23:16, 71–72

Jericho, 180

Jerusalem: Babylonian sack of, 68; exile from, lamenting, 83; pilgrimage to, 22, 23, 107, 108

Jesuit motto, 24

Jesuits, 21, 22, 45, 46, 164, 173–174, 194*n*3

Jesus: as a baby, 156; blind men calling out to, story of, 180–181; on the cross, echoing the words of, 160; death and resurrection of, 4; disciple reclining next to, 154; facing death, 133; famous sermon of, 42, 79; footsteps of, 108; gospel message of, 131, 152; images that portray the Passion of, prayer before, 140; intercessory prayer by, 96; last supper of, 114, 115, 176; Lent modeled after experience of, 105; living and suffering as did, 45; Martha's protest to, 154; pausing to listen to, biblical example of, 154; personal relationship with, worship focused exclusively on, 50; pilgrimage of, to Jerusalem, 107; praying for, to guide the TRC hearings, 89–90; reconciling work of, 97; responding to Martha, 154–155; Satan's tempting of, 19; spirituality in solidarity with, 46; Taizé music about, 151, 152; teaching the disciples, 9, 78, 85, 98, 118, 165–166; view that prolife movement defies the teachings of, 132; wariness of, 118

Jesus Prayer, the, 18, 178

Jews: edict expelling, from Rome, 73; offering refuge to, fleeing Nazi rule, 148; as prochoice supporters, 128; walking with Our Lady of Guadalupe banner, 111

Johannesburg, 59, 67, 81, 89

John: 13:23, 154; 13:25, 154; 17:9-23, 96; 17:24, 96

1 John 4:1, 72

Jonah, 113, 114; 3:5, 113; 3:8, 113

Judeo-Christian tradition, resources from, 13–14. *See also specific traditions*

Judson Memorial Church, 54

Justice and Peace Committee, 37, 38, 39, 40–41, 42, 43

Justice and Witness Ministries, 36

Justice's urgency, 53

K

Kairos Document, The, 68–69, 70

Kerry, J., 1

King, M. L., Jr., 99

Kirchner, J., 111

Knock, pilgrimage to, 108

Korea, quiet witness in, 148

L

Lament: over apartheid's injustice, 82–87, 170–171; over deaths at abortion clinic, 139; over Roe v. Wade decision, 126–128; path of, 170–171; slowly repeating psalm of, 178

Last Supper, the, 114, 115, 154. *See also* Eucharist, the

Latin America, struggle for liberation in, 45–48

Latino community, attempt to organize, in California, 101

"Laudate Omnes Gentes, Laudate Dominum" song, 145

Layoffs, response to, questioning, xiii

Lectio divina, 150–151, 177–179

Lent, 105, 114, 174

Lesbian and gay marriage/unions, 1, 34, 50–51

Liberal Christians, 1, 2, 34, 48

Liberation, struggle for: in Latin America, 45–48; in South Africa, 58, 80–81, 86

Liberation theologians, 45–46, 47, 48

Life: as a community of prayer, 5; of prayer, 147–152; the term, refusal to surrender, to the prolife movement, 129; views on, 127, 129, 136

Life of Christ, 22

Listening, time for, 153, 154

Liturgy of the Hours, saying the, 7

Living generously, example of, 21–25

Long Night's Journey into Day, 94

Lord's Prayer, The, 9, 65, 72, 78, 165, 166

Los Angeles district of United Methodist churches, 130

Los Angeles Planned Parenthood chapter, 131

Lough Derg, pilgrimage to, 109–110
Lourdes, pilgrimage to, 108
Love of neighbor, 21, 79, 90
Lowney, S., 129, 137, 138, 139
Luke: 2:41-42, 107; 10:38-42, 154; 10:40, 154; 10:41, 154–155; 11:1, xv; 11:4, 78; 11:9-10, 9–10
Lutheran prolife supporters, 127

M

Macarius, 17, 18, 165
Mandela, N., 67, 87, 88, 93
Manhattan, West Side of, quiet witness in, 148
March for Life, 126, 127–128, 136
Mark: 11:1-11, 107; 11:24, 85; 11:25, 85–86; 14:23, 115
Marriage: defined, by the Church, 50; same-sex unions and, 1, 34, 50–51
Martha, 154, 154–155
Martyrdom, 46
Marxist political ideology, 48
Mary, 4, 127, 156. *See also* Virgin Mary, the
Mary of Bethany, 153–154
Mass: attending, 100, 115, 126, 127, 136; prayer during, 50–51, 175–176; self-serving behavior after, 117
Massachusetts: attack on Planned Parenthood clinic in, 137; debate over same-sex marriage in, 50, 51
Matthew: 4:1-11, 19; 5:44, 79; 6:5-6, 132; 6:7-8, 166; 6:9-13, 9; 6:17-18, 118; 7:15, 72; 19:14, 156; 20:29-34, 180–181; 25:40, 41
McCarrick, 126
Mecca, pilgrimage to, 107
Meditation, 19, 29, 139, 153, 156
Mercy, praying for, 2, 165, 180–181
Messiah complex, 112

Messiness: of choices, 10; of politics, 48
Methodist churches, 41, 50, 66, 67, 81, 130
Mexican Catholicism, 100–101, 102, 103
Mexican culture, 113
Mexican immigrants, 100. *See also* Farm workers
Mexican Independence Day, 102
Mexico City, 102
Mexico, patron saint of, 103
Mhlawuli, S., 77–78, 80
Miami, Florida, story of church tensions in, 33–55
Miami Herald, 35
Miami police, 37, 38
Micah 6:8, 44, 125, 178
Middle Ages, the, 29
Migrant farm workers, boycott to support, church backing, 39–42. *See also* Farm workers
Militarism, 53
Mississippi Burning, 93
Mkonto, S., 77–78, 80
Mkwayi, I., 87
Monastic communities, 7, 26
Montgomery, Alabama, 99
Morality, upholding, issue of, 1
Music and singing in the Taizé community, 150, 151–152, 153, 156, 158, 159
Muslims, 107
Mystery, 164

N

Nahuatl language, 102
National Council of Churches, 41–42
National Council of Churches of Christ in the USA, 138
National Farm Worker Association (NFWA), 99, 111
National Farm Worker Ministry, 39

National Network of Abortion
Funds, 129
National treasury, giving away
the, to the rich, 54
Nazi rule: offering refuge to Jews
fleeing, 148; resistance to, 74
Neighbors, loving one's, 21, 79, 90
Nero, 73
New England Annual Conference
of the United Methodist
Church, 50
New Testament copies, distribu-
tion of, in Russia, 149
New Year's, 158
New York Avenue Presbyterian
Church, 128–129
New York City church, 54
New York hospital, 124
News, praying with the, 178–179
Nichols, L., 129, 137, 138, 139
Nineveh, 113, 114
"Nkosi Sikelela iAfrika" (God bless
Africa) anthem, 79, 81–82, 85
No Future Without Forgiveness
(Tutu), 95
Nobel Peace Prize, 87
Nonviolence, movements holding
to, importance of, 104–105,
107, 112, 113, 114, 174
North American Free Trade
Agreement (NAFTA), 36
Northern Ireland community, 7–8

O

Open Forum, 37, 38
Orendain, T., 112
Our Lady of Guadalupe: building
shrines to, 117; farm workers
walking with, 99, 100,
104–107, 111; prolife supporters walking with, 127;
reverence for, 101; story of,
102–103; as a symbol, 103
Our Lady of Guadalupe church,
102

P

Passivity, wrongly justifying, 47
Passover, 107, 115, 176
Pastoral candidate, ideal, one
church's description of, 55
Pastoral Epistle, 62
Pastors and politics, issue of, 12,
35, 43, 48–52
Patrick, St., 109
Patriotism, 54
Paul, 3–4, 5, 18, 62, 71, 73–74, 96,
169, 177
Paul III, 23
Pause button, prayer as a, 6–8
Pavone, F., 139
Peace, 42, 49, 51, 62, 66, 146, 158,
160
Peaceful protest, police violence
erupting during, 59–60
Peach church, 54
Penance, act of, 105, 106, 107, 109,
110, 113, 137, 174, 175. *See
also* Pilgrimage; Repentance
Pensacola, Florida, attack at abor-
tion clinic in, 138
People for the American Way,
38–39
Peregrinación, 105
Personal agendas, using prayer
as a tool to advance, problem
of, xv
Personal privacy, right of, 125
Peruvian theologian, 47
Petitionary prayer: flowing from
certain way of living, 4; questioning, xvii, 10
Pieterson, A., 60
Pieterson, H., 59–60, 76
Pilgrimage: Christian history of,
107–109; farm worker, 12, 99,
105–107, 110–111, 119, 174;
Irish, 109–110; to Jerusalem,
22, 23, 107, 108; prolife,
135–137; of trust on earth,
158–159

Planned Parenthood: clergy advisory board of, 123; Los Angeles chapter of, 131; national chaplain of, 130–132; religious support for, and alliances with, 130

Planned Parenthood clinics: attack on, 137; prayer together outside, yet divided in belief, example of, 141–142; protests at, 121–122, 136. *See also* Abortion clinics

Pleins, J. D., 84

Polarized prayers, 137–141

Police, the, 37, 38, 59–60, 78, 81, 91, 92

Political prayer calling for change. *See* Prophetic prayer

Politics: pastors and, issue of, 12, 35, 43, 48–52; spirituality and, xiv, 12, 33–55, 64, 66, 69, 76, 83, 118, 119, 167. *See also* Government; Social action

Port Elizabeth, South Africa, 77

Power: and ambiguity, 28–31; of prayer, 85, 169

Prayer: Jesus teaching about, 9, 78, 85, 98; paths of, 170–180; power of, 85, 161, 169. *See also specific type of prayer and prayerful situations*

Prayer of the Faithful, 50–51, 127

Presbyterian Church (USA), 41, 128–129

Presbyterian minister, defrocked, 138

Presidential candidates, looking at, from various perspectives, 1–2

Presidential Prayer Team, 59

Presumptuous prayer, 67, 71, 76

Priests for Life, 135, 139–140, 141

"Principle and Foundation" examen, 194*n*3

Privacy, personal, right of, 125

Prochoice movement: and the civil rights movement, 124; issue of ceding *choice* to the, 126–127; leading voice of the clergy in, 123; prayer at the heart of, 138–139, 140–141; threat of violence pressing in on, 137–138

Prochoice supporters: clergy speaking out as, 129–132; demonstrations by, 122; entering into the story of, 12; and expression of solidarity, 133; marking the anniversary of Roe v. Wade, 125, 128–129; reason for view of, example of, 123–124; view of, 123

Prolife movement: condemnation of, 132; issue of surrendering *life* to the, 129; prayer at the heart of, 139–140, 141

Prolife supporters: demonstrations by, 121–122, 124–125, 176; entering into the story of, 12; and expression of solidarity, 133; marking the anniversary of Roe v. Wade, 125, 126–128; pilgrimage by, 135–137; and prayer outside abortion clinics, 132–135; reason for view of, example of, 124–125; student response to, xvii; view of, 122–123

Prophecy and spirituality, 119

Prophetic movement, 131

Prophetic prayer: calling for, 60–63; under a democracy, issue of, 58–59; and discernment, 72, 75–76, 172; and issue of obedience to the government, 73–75; as rejecting the status quo, 63–65; spirit behind, 67–72; vision of, 57–58; voices of caution concerning, 65–67

Prophetic role, church living
out a, 61
Protest, prayerful. *See* Raised fists,
praying with
Protestant California Migrant
Ministry, 116
Protestant Reformers, 111
Protestants and Catholics: conflict between, seeking
reconciliation for, 7–8;
contemplative community
composed of, 146, 148; in
shared prayer, but with different convictions on abortion, 141–142; walking with
Our Lady of Guadalupe
banner, 111
Psalms: 44:5-6, 171; 44:9-11, 83;
44:23, 83–84, 171, 178; 44:24,
171; 44:26, 84, 171; 70:1, 19;
84:1-5, 107; 131:1-2, 179;
137:9, 85
Psalms, the: chanting of, by
desert elders, 19; of lament,
83–85, 170–171, 178; singing
of, in monastic communi-
ties, 7
Public prayer: dangers of, 132,
167; need for, acknowledging, 166; questioning, 143
Puerto Rico, 123
Pulpit Search Committee, 55

Q

Quaker writer, 118
Questions: big, hesitancy to ask,
9; entering into the, 11; facing our, 8; words giving voice
to, 84
Quiet witness, 146, 148

R

Race riots, 100
Racial discrimination, legislation
outlawing, 100

Racial ethnicity of church members, in Coral Gables,
184–185*n*1
Racial segregation and discrimina-
tion, official system of, 58.
See also Apartheid
Rahner, K., 164–165, 171
Raised fists, praying with, 80–82,
83, 85, 86, 97, 171. *See also*
Lament
Reagan, R., 101
Recessional hymn, 127
Reconciliation: community seek-
ing, in Northern Ireland,
7–8; concern for, 157; form-
ing bonds of, 158; ground of,
147; quiet witness for peace
and, 146, 148; in South
Africa, 12, 78, 79–80, 87,
87–90, 89, 90, 91, 94, 97
Reconciliation church, 145, 146,
149–150, 155–156, 160
Reflection, 22, 24
Reformation, the, 22
Reformed churches, 60–61, 63–64,
93, 94
Reformed theologian, 74–75
Reformers, 111
Regularity, importance of, 7
Relationship: personal, with Jesus,
worship focused exclusively
on, 50; prayer as, 26
Religious Coalition for Abortion
Rights, 130
Religious Coalition for Repro-
ductive Choice, 129–130,
140–141
Religious spirituality. *See*
Spirituality
Remorse, expressing, 93
Repentance, 89, 93, 113, 114, 116,
139, 140. *See also* Penance,
act of
Repetition, 18, 19, 150, 152
Republicans, 34

Resting, time for, 153, 154
Restless life, 108–109
Retreat guide, 23, 24
Rhythm, importance of, 7
Robben Island, 67
Roe v. Wade, 124, 125, 126–129, 140
Roger, 145, 149, 150, 158, 160, 161, 179
Roman Catholic archdiocese, Boston, 50
Roman Catholic prolife group, 136
Roman Catholic standpoint, looking at presidential candidates from, 2
Roman Empire, 20
Roman rule, letter about living under, 62
Romans: 8:26, 71; 8:26-27, 169; 13, 73, 75; 13:1-2, 74; 16, 74
Romans, the, letter to, 71, 73–74, 169
Rome, pilgrimage to, 108
Romero, O., 46
Rosary, protestors reciting the, 122
Ross, B., 49
Ross, F., 101
Roundtables: imaginary, 163–164, 181; real, need for more, 168–169
Royal Dutch/Shell, 42
Rule, the, 7, 150
Russell, P., 66
Russia, ties of the Taizé community to, 149
Russian peasant/pilgrim, 19, 178

S

Sacramento, California, 99, 105, 110, 111
St. John the Devine Cathedral, 137, 139
Saint Patrick's Purgatory, 109
Salvadorians, murder of, 46
Salvi, J., 137

Same-sex marriage/unions, 1, 34, 50–51
Samuel, 71
1 Samuel 1:15, 71
San Jose, California, 101
Sanctuary, politics in the, 48–52
Sanderson, S., 129
Saratoga Hospital, New York, 124
Satan (the devil), 19, 27
Schaper, D., 35, 36, 37, 38, 39, 44, 48–49, 52–54, 167
Schenley Corporation, 111
Schutz, G., 148
Schutz, R., 147–148
Scripture reading. See Bible reading
Secret fasting, 118
Secret prayer, 132
Self-abandonment, 164, 165
Self-deception, 10, 29, 72, 142, 165
Self-serving behavior, fasting and, 116–117, 118
Selma, Alabama, 99
Senegal, quiet witness in, 148
"Senzenina" ("What Have We Done?") hymn, 91, 97–98
Seoul, Korea, quiet witness in, 148
Serenity, divine, sharing in, 95–97, 179
Sermon on the Mount, 42, 79
Silence: appropriateness of, 166; cultivating, 165; last moment before, 164, 165; in monastic communities, 7; in the Taizé community, 150, 153, 156, 158, 159
Silvanus, 4
Simple prayer, 2, 165, 166, 181
Singing and music in the Taizé community, 150, 151–152, 153, 156, 158, 159
Slepian, B., 129
Sobrino, J., 45–46
Social action: call to, pastor's growing sense of, 53–54;

integration of prayer and, complexity of, 11; as a mission, 52, 173; relationship between prayer and, ambiguity over, 20, 30–31; springing from and reflecting Christian faith, 5, 167. *See also* Action; Politics

Social action groups, 3

Social activist pastor, 35

Social activists, reminder of hope for, 8

Social Ethics in Business, 194*n*3

Social justice committee, xv

Social justice, community articulating its mission in terms of, 173–174

Social welfare funding, expanding, 1

Socially active congregational community, 34

Solidarity: issue of, in the abortion debate, 133; with Jesus, spirituality in, 46; prayer as deep expression of, 177

Solitude, 20, 21, 22, 23, 29

South Africa: amnesty in, 88, 91, 93, 94, 190*n*20; black national anthem of, 79, 81–82; struggle for liberation in, 58. *See also* Apartheid in South Africa

South African Council of Churches (SACC), 60, 61–62, 81, 86

South African police, 59–60, 78, 91, 92

South African theologians, 63, 64, 68, 74, 91

South African widows, 78, 79, 80, 90, 93–94

Southern Baptists, 50

Soweto Uprising, 59–60, 61, 76

Spanish conquest, the, 102

Spanish Inquisition, 27, 157

Spiritual, being, questioning what defines, 43–48

Spiritual Exercises, The (Ignatius of Loyola), 23, 24

Spiritual life committee, xv

Spiritual training, 174–175

Spiritual warfare, prolife supporters engaged in, 134–135

Spirituality: authentic, 164; confusion about, 30; false, 46, 69; false separation of, from theology, 29; Ignatian, 14, 24, 25, 173–174, 194–195*n*3; and politics, xiv, 12, 33–55, 64, 66, 69, 76, 83, 118, 119, 167; prophecy and, 119; in solidarity with Jesus, 46; status quo, rejecting, 63–65. *See also* Faith

Stability of church members, in Coral Gables, 185*n*1

"Stations of the cross" Catholic devotion, 140

Status quo spirituality, rejecting, 63–65

Status quo, the: passive acquiescence to, 154; questioning the, 172

Stebbins, J. M., 194*n*3

Stem cell research, xiii, 10

Stevens, D., 7–8

Stillness, 5–6, 95, 179. *See also* Contemplation; Meditation

Storey, P., 66–67, 81

Strikes, 102, 104, 105, 118

Structural sin, knowingly or unknowingly participating in, 173

Student protest movement, 100, 104–105

Stylite, S., 20

Success, cultural measure of, 5

T

Taco Bell, boycott against, church backing, 39–42

Taizé community, 12–13, 145–161, 194*n*13

Tarshish, 113

Taylor, E., 91, 92–93, 94, 95

Teamsters union, 101

Teichert, J., 136–137

Temple, the: destruction of, lamenting, 83; pilgrimage to, 107

Tepeyac, hill of, 102, 103

Teresa of Avila, 14, 25–28, 29, 30, 153, 156–157

Thanksgiving, prayer in a context of, 4

Theology, false separation of spirituality from, 29

Thessalonians, the, Paul's exhortation to, 177

1 Thessalonians: 3:8, 3; 3:10, 4; 5:16-18, 4

Timothy, 4

1 Timothy: 1:17, 63; 2, 74, 75; 2:1-3, 62

Totalitarianism, 74

Traditional Catholics, in Mexico, 100–101, 102, 103

Tragic day, remembering a, 59–60, 76

True fasts, 174–175

True prayer, 68, 142–143, 166, 175

Trust: forging bonds of, 146, 148–149, 158; full of, 164, 165; and humility, as integral, 18; in prophetic prayer, 71; wellsprings of, going to the, 157–160, 179

Truth and Reconciliation Commission (TRC), 79–80, 88, 89, 90, 91, 94, 97, 190n20

Truth, question of, prayer noting, 51

Tutu, D., 80, 86–87, 88–90, 90–91, 94, 95–96, 97, 167, 179

U

"Ubi Caritas," 151

Ubuntu, 97

Unborn, prolife view of the, 133

Unceasing prayer, 4, 18, 19

Uncertainty, 25

Unitarian Universalist leader, 138

United Church of Christ (UCC), 35, 36, 41, 42, 43, 51, 123

United Farm Workers (UFW), 101, 102, 115

United Methodist Church, 41, 50, 130

United Nations, 43

U.S. Constitution, 125

U.S. Supreme Court, 124, 127, 130, 137, 176

Unity: of the Christian community, division in the, 141–143, 148; concern for, 52–53, 157; praying for, 96–97

Unity Committee, 52

University of Central America, 46

Unpatriotic, being labeled as, 54

V

Valdez, L., 106–107

Vengeance, cry for, 85, 86

Ventura Planned Parenthood, 136

Veronica, 140

Veterans Day, 49

Via cruces ("way of the cross"), 108

Vietnam War, the, 35, 100

Villa-Vicencio, C., 64, 65

Violence: police, 59–60, 78; response to, questioning, xiii; unintentionally inciting, concern over, 58, 65–66

Virgin Mary, the: appearance of, 102, 103; icon of, 156; statue of, 23. *See also* Our Lady of Guadalupe

Vyvlecka, S., 136

W

Wade, Roe v., 124, 125, 126–129, 140

Waiting, contemplation involving, 153

213

Index

War: horrible realities of, grappling with, 179; undeclared, 54. *See also specific war*

Washington, D.C.: demonstrations in, 126–128, 128–129, 176; Jesuit theological center in, 194–195*n*3; pilgrimage to, 135–137

Wasson, R., 37

Watts race riots, 100

"Way of the cross" (*via cruces*), 108

Way of the Pilgrim, The (Anonymous), 19

Weber, M., 48

Western culture, contemporary, 5–6

Weyrich, M. T., 124–125

White House, the, 127

Withdrawal. *See* Solitude

Witness: quiet, for peace and reconciliation, 146, 148; viewing prayer as, in a prolife pilgrimage, 135–137; wrestling with the, 119

Witnesses, cloud of, 17–31, 95–97

Woman pastor, breaking ground as a, 35

Women's Fund of Western Massachusetts, 54

Women's rights, protection of, 128, 131

Woodstock Theological Center, 194–195*n*3

World Alliance of Reformed Churches, 60–61

World War II, 146, 147, 148

Worship, false, 68

Worship services, pastoral preaching and prayers for, politics and, 48–52

Y

Yale University, 35

Youth Mass for Life, 126, 129